FEAR NOT,

FOR HE IS WITH US!

Fear fades as Faith grows and when
Faith grows you have Hope.
—Romans 10:17

Do not fear for I am with you.
—Isaiah 41:10

Brenda Carlisle Porter

ISBN 978-1-0980-6731-1 (paperback)
ISBN 978-1-0980-6733-5 (hardcover)
ISBN 978-1-0980-6734-2 (digital)

Christian Faith Publishing, Inc.
832 Park Avenue
Meadville, PA 16335
www.christianfaithpublishing.com

Printed in the United States of America

I dedicate this book to our Lord, who answers prayers and works miracles, not once on me but lots of times. If it were not for Him, there would be no story to be told.

Also, to the loving memory of my father, George Wesley Carlisle, who is in heaven, and my mother, Alice Carlisle, who is an angel on earth.

I dedicate this to my wonderful husband, Gary, whom I love very much. I am so blessed to be his wife. I am a better person because of his love and faith.

I dedicate this also to my wonderful children and grandchildren. You are so precious to me. I thank God for you every day, and I love you with all my heart.

I dedicate this to Gary's mom, Berlene Brandon, who is in heaven with my father.

I dedicate this book to all my friends, family, and churches. Thank you all for your prayers during my struggles. Thank you for standing by me and your support of me through everything.

Thank you very much from the bottom of my heart. I love you all.

God's Plan for Me to Share My Story

God has a plan for me in His own timing, and because of His healing, He got me through it. I now commit my life to Him. I want to witness constantly and please God. I want to write this book for Him and witness my story to others. He is the center of my life. I want to always remember that I only have to please one person. If what I do pleases God, it is always the right thing to do. I can stop worrying about everyone else's reactions and not be manipulated by disapproval from others. God shaped me to be me, not someone else.

I do feel like I have succeeded in life by being the Christian I am. I have always wanted to have a strong faith mentally, physically, and spiritually. God has given me a miracle by being here, which gives me happiness, joy, and peace.

I want to share with others what He did for me and let them know He can do the same for them. In my mind, this seems so far out. I never thought I could even think of writing a book. I just want to witness to everyone. I truly believe God gave me another chance so I can witness.

I started this book in 2009. I'm still at it. I see that God is with me constantly while writing this book. I feel Him. I remember the difficult time. God gave me strength. It looked dark. I didn't think I'd see another happy day. God turned it around and gave me joy.

Over the years, I have been so blessed by miracles the Lord has given me that I feel in my heart the reason I am here is to write this book and witness to give back to Him. I need to affect and not infect this world. I need to witness to all.

I hope as you read the book you will share it with other's. This will be your way of witnessing also. The Lord wants us to share His gospel through our life to bring people closer to Him. You may experience a struggle in your life that you need Him to be with you to get you through it as I did. It's not too late to start a relationship with Him today.

Remember, it's not the religion you have; it's the relationship you have with Him. I pray this book will give you a better insight of becoming closer to God.

I have learned a lot of people do not know Him. They don't understand the reason why we should worship Him and the powerful impact that praising Him has on our lives. People that know God understand Him. We don't really know how to worship God until we become to know Him by having a closer relationship with Him. Every time we praise and worship God, we understand more about who He is. To worship God is a gift God gives us. It is a means of finding a purpose in our life. We begin to understand who we are by having a relationship with Him.

Gary and Brenda Porter

Thank you for all your love and support. You are why I am the person I am today through your goodness, honesty, and faith.

Contents

Preface

WHY READ THIS BOOK

I hope that by reading this book, you will experience blessings (hope, happiness, prosperity, fulfillment, and understanding). It is my prayer that you experience this book's truths spiritually, mentally, and physically. I hope as you read this book, you gain a broader understanding and obtain more faith by acting on God's promises and be healed. Regardless of what your past or future holds, you will laugh, and you will cry as you walk through the healing journey of this book. This book will encourage you to have hope to empower you to take charge of your life and healing process.

I went through many things in my journey God had for me. I faced a wide variety of obstacles. On the way, I have climbed mountains and went into valleys. Some were rough, and some were smooth. It was hot, muggy, and tiring. I had joy and sorrow, heartaches and anxiety. I had pain, and I had tears. I focused my efforts on trying to rise above them. At times I rested from the battle, and at times I had peace from the storm.

In this book, I am sharing my testimonies of my life before and after cancer. I wrote what I am grateful for, and I wrote prayers straight from my heart. My life is a story, and I want to fill these pages with the stories of the blessings the Lord has given me. Each day, I get to write a new page.

When I look back, I see more clearly His plan for me. I'm so glad I kept my faith and let the Lord carry me through this instead of trying to do it myself. Christ has made a difference in my life, and I feel like sharing this book with you will draw you closer to Him. It's all the truth, and the truth is what God wants us to tell. By God giving me joy in my life, He can give you joy also. My hope is that this book will provide encouragement, strength, and inspiration to overcome whatever challenges you face in life. God is here for you. We make the choice to do the things we want to do. Always make the choice to put your complete trust and confidence in Him and His Word. He took care of me, and He will do it for you.

Everyone wants to live on top of the mountain, but all the growth occurs while you're climbing it. We cannot see the road ahead because of all the obstacles, but once you are on top of the mountain, it is great.

This is a very powerful book. Your whole outlook on life can be changed. You will love reading testimonies that the Lord has pre-formed, and the powerful words of healing will also become reality to you as you read it. It can be a life-changing event if you are going through a hardship and need support and hope. It can help you and your children grow spiritually and become more secure as a family. Many people have gotten closer to the Lord and have received blessings from it.

I pray this book will inspire you to fight obstacles in your life and comfort you in times of pain and suffering. I hope it will open guidance in your life and be a wake-up call for those of you who are facing battles. I hope this book gives you faith, hope, and courage to win the battle. I pray this book will provide encouragement, strength, and peace to overcome whatever challenges you may be facing in your life. I pray your strength will be stronger than ever. Always know that God is with you every minute through your journey.

Everyone has problems, and sooner or later, we will all face difficulties and challenges, which are hard to cope with. Always know that God works for the good of those who love Him.

Satan is the author of sickness, disease, and pain, and God is the author of life and health. Just believe and have faith that God said, "I am the Lord who heals you" (Exodus 15:26). Because God said this—and God cannot lie—then healing is yours. It is so important to pray and rebuke the devil; trust in the Lord; read the Bible; have faith; don't worry; honor Jesus's name; learn His Word; rely on the Lord for His healing, His timing, and His plan.

One day, you're going through life, thinking everything's normal. You're good with God, and your faith is strong. But then you hear the word "cancer." Next you hear your husband's job went down, and to add to that, your dad dies. Suddenly you're not quite as sure about prayer and faith as you were before. These are called doubts. Some Christians might tell you that you shouldn't have these, but that's not what the Bible tells us. Doubts are normal as long as you don't hold on to them forever.

Our lives are under assault, not by God but by Satan. The Bible tells us that Satan is the enemy who comes to destroy, steal, and to kill.

Jesus says in John 10:10 (NIV), "The thief comes only to steal and kill and destroy; I have come that they may have life, and have it to the full." Therefore, we need to have strength from our God. Trust Him, and pray for His strength. By doing this, we need to be calm. By doing this, replace fear with confidence, replace worry with faith in Him, and have peace in the midst of trouble.

It is our choice to go to the Lord with our doubts and fears. We don't understand why bad things happen to good people. Being a Christian doesn't mean bad things won't happen, but it does mean that God will be with you when they do.

If you are sick, God wants to heal you. Try not to put doubt in your mind. If there is doubt, then perfect faith cannot exist. You may not be healed unless you have faith. It is your choice to believe and know that God wants to heal you. It is not God's will for you to be sick. It is God's desire to heal you. Life can be tough, but with the Lord on our side, He will help us deal with it.

At a time like this we have to allow our faith to grow by asking God for help. A lot of us decide we don't need God, and we don't want Him to help us. You do need God, more now than ever.

Know that fear and faith have something in common. They both ask us to believe something will happen that we cannot see. Fear says, "Believe the negative." When negative thoughts come, don't let it take root. Just switch over into faith. That is choosing faith instead of fear.

I started this journal in 2009 after I was diagnosed with lung cancer. As I went through it, the Lord gave me courage, strength, and hope to keep me going. It has been ten years now, and I am cancer free. It has been a journey. I know that the Lord has been with me through it all. He gave me hope and carried me through His healing process each time. In 1970, He gave me His perfect healing; in 1990, He gave me His perfect timing; and in 2008, He gave me His perfect plan. I pray that you will discover God's blessings and favor in amazing ways. As of today, I am healthy and happy.

When I was diagnosed with cancer, my daughter was pregnant with my granddaughter. I prayed and asked God to please be with me and give me time to enjoy my grandchildren. I prayed to God that if He did, I will continue to witness constantly for Him. That is why I'm writing this book. I now have four grandchildren that I'm so blessed to have. Knowing that the Lord is the one who worked miracles on me makes my relationship even stronger, and there are so many non-Christians in this world that need witnessing to. God is calling me to witness and assuring me that He will be with me as I write this book.

Non-Christians need to see what God has done for me, and He can do it for them. God gives all of us the power to witness to others. I really feel this. He doesn't care if we try and fail. He wants us to use our talents for Him. He looks at our biggest mistakes as playing it safe, taking no risks, and doing nothing with what He has given us. God wants to give us the strength to stand firm while He works through us to make a difference in this world.

I want to let God do His work through me—to lead, guide, and direct me in His footsteps and image—and I'm sure you do also. Adam and Eve disobeyed God when they chose not to obey Him by eating from the tree. He did not force them to obey Him; He wanted to let them choose to obey Him. They chose to disobey God. This choice was the first sin, and it opened the door for all sin to enter into the world.

Don't use your energy to worry. Choose to obey God. If you turn your problems over to the Lord, He will handle them. Don't try to handle it yourself. Use your energy to believe.

I know it is hard not to fear, but in the long run, having a strong faith will get you through hard times mentally and physically for a better outcome. Worry is a conversation you have with yourself about things you cannot change. Prayer is a conversation you have with God about things He can change. I realize now as I grow older, I look back on my circumstance with this disease, and I see the hand of God in it. As a Christian, you never face the journey alone. In the midst of all this journey, I praised, worshiped, and honored God. I had faith the whole time that He will get me through this. I kept my trust that the Lord will take care of me, and He did. The love of the Lord never ends. Trials make us stronger and shows us who we are in God. Let God lead you through it, and keep your eyes and mind focused on His promise.

Let me help you see reality of what He has in store for you. I want to make an influence and positive contribution by my witnessing. As I said before, it's your choice. God has a plan for your life and a purpose for your future. When something befalls us, it's hard to understand how anything good can come from it. We won't always see it, but know that God is with us, and He will take care of you. He promised to never leave you or forsake you. No matter what you've been through or what's been done to you, if you're still breathing, God isn't finished with you yet.

I never gave up. I tried to be positive and ask God to heal me. I am a lung-cancer survivor. I thank God for my time here. I'm on the top of the world. I appreciate life more than ever. I appreciate everything so much more now. I see life differently. I love life. I'm enjoying the mountaintop to its fullest. I continue to worship God daily. I thank Him every day and every minute for His blessings to me. He has given me another chance and more time on this wonderful earth. Everything is so much more appreciated. Something as simple as going to Starbucks in the morning, I thank God I am here to enjoy it. I never take life for granted anymore. Jesus has made a difference in my life. Lots of people say, "Your faith is a personal, private thing." In the Bible, the people told their personal stories and the part Jesus played in them. No one expects you to have all the answers, but everyone can tell his or her story!

Help me to spread the good news. Tell your friends about this book so they will be blessed. You may help them to become closer to the Lord with a stronger relationship and being healed by reading this book. Also, pray for our nation. We as Americans need to get closer to the Lord instead of further away. "God, please be with our country. Help us to grow closer to thee." Amen. God bless America, and America, bless God!

Prayer

Lord, we thank You for the truth of Your Word. Lord, I have worked on this awesome book for months now. We thank You that as we read Your Word, we will experience Your joy and peace through this book. We ask that You use it to minister to each of our hearts by encouraging us with Your blessings and our future.

Father, I thank You that I am strong with Your Word, and I pray for each one reading this book to become even stronger in Your Word. I trust, Lord, that something has been said to show Your words and that Your Holy Spirit has brought a light in the hearts of each of us to begin to intervene through us Your excitement and hope for our future.

Father, we glorify You because we have hope in You. We know that no matter what happens, You have a plan for us and, You have provided that so we shall go to be with You forever.

You told us in Your Word that when we are saved, we pass from death into life. You told us in Your Word that when You give to us eternal life, we shall never perish.

Oh, help us, heavenly Father to go out and witness Your Word to many. Help us, Lord, to be faithful to the Word of God and understand what it means and apply it to our own lives.

We give You thanks, honor, and glory. We pray these things in Your name. Amen.

Without faith it is impossible to please him; for they that come to God must believe that He is, and that He is a rewarder of them that diligently seek him. (Hebrews 11:6)

If you live in me, and my words live in you, ask what you will and it shall be done to you. (John 15:7)

The Lord is good; His mercy is everlasting, and His truth endures to all generations. (Psalm 100:5)

Come, you children, listen to me; I will teach you the fear of the Lord. (Psalm 34:11)

Faith comes by hearing the word of God. (Romans 10:17)

* * * * *

Today, I feel at peace. Psalm 46—showed me how to be still and trust God to heal my body and spirit and to have a stronger faith!

Thank you Jesus, family, and friends for sticking by me with your help, love, support, and prayers during this time. I am so blessed. Amen!

My husband Gary and I pray together, and that is why we stay together!

<<Note to layout: insert image here>>

Acknowledgments

The experience of this book has been so rewarding. I cannot begin to express all the love shown to me during this illness and treatments. My family and friends were so supportive. I received 387 cards in the first four months after my diagnoses. I could not believe it. I received telephone calls, e-mails, text, gifts, prayers, cards, letters constantly. There were churches all over the whole world praying for me. I was on their prayer list. My husband and children were with me at all doctor appointments. I am well loved, and I know it. I thank God for all of you.

"Thank you, Lord." Without the good Lord, I could not have gone through this. "Lord, thank you for my healing. Lord, I know what you have done for me through all of this. I will always witness for you till I die. You are in control, and I pray to always let You be in control instead of me trying to do it. You have given me a peace through this. Thank You for my family and friends supporting me."

"Thank you to my family, friends and churches, loved ones, and strangers that prayed for me." God comforts us in all our troubles so that we can comfort others. We need each other, even when we're weak and sick from cancer. We allow a friend to take care of us by bringing a meal for our family or sitting with us during a treatment; we provide them with the joy of giving. Friends and family are a blessing. God used our problems not only for the benefit of our faith, but our family and friends as well. It is in life's toughest moments that God's people rally to one another like no group of people any-where on earth. Their love, prayers, cards, calls, devotion, gifts, acts of mercy are incredible. I think back upon those days. Through them, I carried a positive attitude and kept my faith. I always looked at my bracelet—"Fear not for I am with you." I have never felt so loved and so prayed for as I did during those months. God's people bombarded heaven with prayers on my behalf, and God answered their prayers.

Thank you to my parents. I was blessed to be born and raised in a faith-filled home. My mother and father, George and Alice Carlisle, instilled in my sisters and me faith and values that we possess to this day. My parents believed in us. We are thankful for the foundation they provided and for always being there to pick us up when we fell. They never let us down.

Thank you to my husband. God gave me a wonderful husband, Gary, who takes care of me. He has been beside me all the way. He helped me toward wellness. He was with me when my hair left. He held me. He always drove me to the doctor. He always came when I needed him. When I forgot why I was fighting, he reminded me. He let me cry, and he cried with me. He stood with me all the way. While he was working so hard to support me, he took the time out and called me every day to make sure I was okay. He put me before his job. He walked the darkness with me. He gave me gifts of love and encouragement. God assisted my husband and me in our financial needs through this sickness and Gary's business closing down.

Here are some other words of comfort given to me during my journey with cancer.

My daughter Lisa called me one day and said, "Mama, I found this in the Bible. Please write it down and adhere to it, and I did: "Trust in the Lord with all your heart and lean not on your own understanding in all your ways, acknowledge Him and He will make your path straight."

My mama Alice constantly told me this during my treatment: "All things are possible with the Lord. The same God that helped you find it will cure you." She called me and prayed with me every day. My daddy George said, "Brenda, I'm always here for you, and I love you."

My sister Vicki: "Brenda, keep saying, 'I can do all things through God, who is my strength.'" She was there and has been my whole life, supporting and comforting me. She worked with the airlines and had every priest she came in contact with pray for me.

My sister Jeanette: "I love you, honey. Hang in there. God is with you always."

Steve, my son: "Mama, the Lord is looking out for you. I just know it. He has a good team of doctors taking care of you."

Michael, my son-in-law: "Hang in there. You will be fine."

Denise, my daughter-in-law: "You are strong. You can conquer this."

Abby, my dog; she curled up close to me in the bed and sit in my lap while in a chair. She knew what I was going through. I could tell when I was sad, she was. When I had a little energy, she did. She never left my side.

My sister Judy gave me a cross to carry with me, and with this cross, she gave me the following saying by Verna Thomas. I carry my cross in my pocket book today.

> I carry a cross in my pocket. A small reminder to me of the fact that I am a Christian, no matter where I may be. This little cross is not magic, nor is it a good luck charm. It isn't meant to protect me from every physical harm. It is not for identification for all the world to see. It's simply an understanding between my savior and me. It reminds me too, to be thankful for my blessings day by day, and to strive to serve Him better in all that I do and say. It's also a daily reminder of the peace and comfort I share, with all who know my master and give themselves to His care. So, I carry a cross in my pocket reminding no one but me, that Jesus Christ is Lord of my life. If only I'll let Him be.

"Thank you, Judy, for all your love, encouragement, and support."

My friend Diane wrote a wonderful letter to me during my time of distress. In the letter, she said, "We serve a faithful Lord!" If we ask Him, He always answers! "Because the Lord helps me, I will not be disgraced. Therefore, I have set my face like a stone, determined to do His will, and I know that I will not be put to shame" (Isaiah 50:7).

She said, "As long as you live on this earth, you will never be free from troubles, but you can have the power to overcome it. When you desire and allow the Holy Spirit to work in you, He will help you overcome. When you begin to see the obstacles in your life as opportunities for God to show His power, they will seem so overwhelming. The hardships and weaknesses that frighten you may be the tools God wants to use to help you overcome. Allow the Holy Spirit today to turn your obstacles into His opportunities."

God has been faithful to us in giving us all we need to get through this life, and He will continue to be faithful as He promised He would. She said she was reading through a book called *Life on the Rails* by Steven Ciezki, and she was blessed with what God was saying, and she wanted to share it with me.

"No temptation [trial/tests] has overtaken you but such as in common to men; and God is faithful, who will not allow you to be tempted beyond what you are able, but with the temptation (trial/test) will provide the way of escape, that you may be able to endure it" (1 Corinthians 10:13). Paul is saying that when we face trials in our life, we can take comfort in knowing that others have and are facing these problems successfully; we are not alone.

But another thing Paul is saying is that God is faithful, who will not allow you to be tempted (tested) beyond what you are able. He knows what we can deal with. He wants us to know that He is there, walking right beside us and only allowing what we can deal with, yet the way we deal with it is understanding that He is in control completely, and we can trust Him because we are His children, and He loves us more than we can ever understand. God will provide a way of escape.

Looking through the eyes of faith, God always provides a way for us to receive adequate help—spiritual, physical, and emotional—to endure our trials. Diane said, "He is with us, Brenda, even these trials that we are enduing. We know God has given us His promise, and we will not be overwhelmed, but we will trust Him and His Word, and we will encourage each other with His promises to us.

Let's cling together to His promise and trust Him through this trial that He has allowed us to walk through for His glory. Together, we will "cast our burdens upon the Lord, and He will sustain us. He will never allow the righteous to be shaken" (Psalm 55:22).

Diane has been my mentor and an inspiration to me. She and I met in Kansas in 1985 and have been close friends since. Through our faith in the Lord, we give each other strength. We have so much in common and love the Lord with all our hearts. Thank you, Diane, for your encouragement.

The list goes on and on from family, friends, and churches. At a time like this, it is so important to feel the strong prayers. I truly believe God listened to all the prayers. You will see later in my book how He was there for me as I was praying on my way to the pharmacy and how an angel gave me a bracelet. He gave me reassurance of my prayer.

Legacy

Suddenly, I am now faced with the fact that I will soon be the oldest generation in my family. My parents were part of what has been known as my "greatest generation." They fell in love before World War II. Daddy had to go to war, and when he returned, they married. They grew up in the depression. They knew what it felt like to be hungry. But in the midst of this, there was lots of love.

I often wonder how they managed to get through those difficult times. My life has been so easy in comparison. With all the things they experienced, they never went to a counselor, never took tranquilizers, and it never limited them as a married couple or as parents. They just put it behind them and went on. Family was most important. Family worked together. Extended family members lived close by and visited often. Some lived under the same roof.

I was born on May 1, 1948. My mother and father were textile workers. They worked hard to take care of my sisters and me. We always felt very safe and secure in our home in the little textile town of Erwin, North Carolina. While young with my parents, they would always make sure my sisters and I were in church. My parents extended the love of God to my sisters and me like a lifeline. They prayed with us and raised us knowing the Lord. As I thought about my life, it struck me that my parents never made me feel unloved. This was an incredible gift.

As a little girl, at church, I didn't understand, but I did hear the Word of the Lord. His words were strong, and if what the Bible said was true, I wanted to know more about it. I remember as a teenager, I would often read the Bible. I could feel the truth and the reality of the Lord. I wanted to receive Jesus and experience the life God had for me. As I grew older, I started to realize for myself who Jesus really is. I could see God's peace and joy.

I go to church to learn more about Him. Every service I go to, I see that even though I am praising God, I am the one being blessed. He fulfills and enriches my life. I learned the importance and power of prayer, worship, and praise. I wanted to worship God. The truth is, when we worship God, it affects who we become as a person. The more we worship God, the more we become like Him, and we become all we are created to be.

As an adult, I look back and I see my faith grew stronger through the years. I pray a lot more now than I did. I realize more than ever that I have to do something kind for myself to keep me and my emotions healthy. I treat myself to a hot bath, or I walk. I do what I can to get emotionally released. I find time with God. I pray and talk to Him. I listen to Christian teachings and Christian music. These always inspire me and make me feel good.

I realized when I was young, I felt I knew a lot, but I didn't know all that much about me, others, the world, and God. It has taken both joy and sorrow, gain and loss to open my eyes. Going through obstacles in my life have been a time of discovery. I am so grateful for my gift of life every day. God has angels looking out for me. He has worked so many miracles on me, and He helped me find my cancer, and He got rid of it. I can trust Him.

As a little girl, my mom always told me I was a born-again Christian. She said when I was five years old, she was worried about Daddy because he had not arrived home, and it was late. When I went to bed, my mom came to my bedside to say a prayer with me. She prayed that Daddy would be home soon. I said to Mom, "Daddy will be fine."

She said, "How do you know, honey?"

I said, "Because in my mind, someone is telling me he is."

My mom at that time knew that was my consciousness talking to me, which was the Lord. He told me so I could relay it to her. Sure enough, right after our prayer, Dad came home and was fine. I have learned over the years that your consciousness is your guide. It can accuse you or excuse you. You know what is right and what is wrong. God just wants you to know His laws and honor them.

I have learned that Christianity is not a religion; it is a relationship and lifestyle. A relationship always requires communication. It's allowing God and Jesus to be in us. Therefore, prayer is essential. Through prayer, I communicate with my Lord. The more I pray and study the Word of God, the stronger my relationship will be with Him. By having the relationship, you will know that He hears our prayers and answers them.

I have learned that everything in God's creation has purpose. God has a purpose for you. Our main purpose is to love Him with our worship and praise. Every time you worship God, you are fulfilling one of your purposes on earth, and you are giving God pleasure.

I stopped and thought about my own life. How will the generations that follow me be influenced by my witnessing? What kind of legacy will I leave my children and grandchildren? Living a good life of integrity and excellence that honors God is worth more than all the riches on earth.

We as parents can leave a family legacy. God has promised that your seed (your family) will live up to a thousand generations. They will have the blessings of God. All because of the life you have lived. You may have a big dream. God may have put this seed in you to get it started. Your children and grandchildren may take it further than you ever thought possible. It is so important for us as a parent to instill in our children to have a close relationship with the Lord and for them to know the love of God. Teach them while young to pray, trust, and have faith in God.

Heavenly Father, I pray that my children and grandchildren will always be led by your Word. May they love you above all else. And may you protect, guide, and lead them through their lives and our generations to come. Amen.

I do know, if a child seems indifferent toward the faith of their parents, just know that God is still at work. Things can change in years to come, and seeds of faith can show up in generations to come.

A lot of my family are Christians. I'm so proud of my past generations. My mom told me her mom (my grandmother) was a born-again Christian. She wrote prayers. She died at my mom's birth. My mom's grandparents raised her. They were Christians also (they were my great-grandparents). My great-great granddaddy was a Methodist preacher. His name was Thomas E. Tart. He had a small church and lots of members. He paid the price to invest in my mom's future, my future, my children's future, and my grandchildren's future. Thank you, Lord, for my family heritage. Amen.

While I was in the hospital with surgery on my lung, my daddy was in another hospital with his last days. My knowledge of having cancer and the procedures were bad, but the event of my daddy's death shook me like no other in my life. I had lost other members of my family before, but I was young, and my life was still ahead of me. I remember grieving the loss of my grandparents when I was young, but I was so immature. I had a husband to find and children to have.

But now, I've gone through years. This was different. I had my daddy so many years. He was ninety-two years old, and I was sixty-one. My dad and I even grew closer as my children married and moved out of our house. I have spent the last years of Daddy's life with him and mama a lot. I prayed with my daddy a lot the last few years of his life. I wanted him to go to heaven. I prayed a Savior's prayer often to him. The Lord says, "Honor thy mother and father," and I feel I have honored the Lord with this. If you honor the Lord, He will get you through any obstacle. And He has proven this over and over again.

Even though I lost my dad during my cancer, my mom is still with me. Thank you, Jesus, for her. I want to be with her every moment. She took care of my granddaddy and my daddy, and I want to take care of her. She is an angel. My sisters and I love her with all our heart. She has been the biggest inspiration in our life. My mom inspires us every day with her faithfulness to our Lord. I want to be a godly person like my mom and let the light shine over my head as an angel.

In Proverbs 11:5, it says that ability will enable a man to go to the top, but it takes character to keep him there. Be a person of God's image by being a godly person. By doing this, we need to be trustworthy, honest, and respectful. I have learned that people will love you more and respect you so much more. You will be a happier person because you will have hope and someone to talk to even in your worst situation that life throws at you. If we are a Christian, we march through this world like a soldier, get knocked down and get up until we look and act like Jesus.

I want to walk in Jesus's footsteps as much as I can. I had rather do and not promise than promise and not do. Your word is everything. I was taught to always keep my promises and to not gossip about others. It is not godly. Gossip is anytime you are talking about someone that you cannot do anything about it. Remember, if someone gossips about someone else, they will gossip about you.

Always share your true feelings inside. Hiding your true feelings keeps you in bondage. Sometimes, we have to confront things to make it better. Pray to God about our situation. We get in touch with what is inside of us and talk to God about it. God gives us feelings, and it is all right to minister to our emotions or to the emotions of other people.

I have always felt so safe and secure with God by going to Him with my problems. My mom always said, "Go to the Lord with everything," and that is what I do and what I want my children to do. I could not imagine life without knowing and having a relationship with the Lord. I could not imagine going through a hard time in my life without asking the Lord to help me. This is what I want my children to experience. I want my children to always be able to turn to the Lord through their hard times also. This cannot be done by force and needs to start at a very young age.

I feel there are three things I was put on this earth to do: (1) to know Christ, (2) to witness for Him, and (3) to put Him in the lives of my children and grandchildren.

On September 7, 1969, I married the man who became an important person in my life and the love of my life—my husband, Gary. One year later, we had a daughter, Lisa Kay, and then sixteen months later, we had a son, Steve. Life is so good.

We lived on a farm in the town of Bunnlevel, North Carolina. We raised our children with fresh vegetable, farm animals, and lots of love. Gary worked a full-time job and farmed on the side. I worked full-time at a school so I could have the summers off to enjoy my family and put up frozen and canned vegetables out of our garden. I can look back now, and it's hard to believe all that I did. Time seems to go so much faster now.

Gary and I have been married forty-seven years and are closer than ever. I thank God I have a Christian leader as a husband that kept us close to the Lord. Gary is a man that my children and I have always looked up to. Why? Because he is a Christian and a God-loving man—the most honest, freehearted, and loving person, husband, and father. He is very caring and giving. That is why he is who he is. Gary is a good example of a husband and a daddy because he believes in the Lord, and with his help, my help, and the help of God, our children will know the Lord and grow a closer relationship with Him.

We have such a strong and secure relationship. Our hearts knit together as we pray together, which makes us have a love through Jesus. God binds us together and gives us strength with a heart-to-heart connection. By both of us having faith, our life has been so enriched.

If your children experience having praying parents, it takes a strong start in your family. God will then do His part by giving you a great marriage and relationship with your children. Gary and I did the best we could do showing our children the right foundation of faith for our Lord. We as parents can show them what's right by the way we use our words and deeds. When they see that—us as parents—life is shaped by a relationship with God in a real way, they will tend to be more open to your influence for God.

I have a calmness of knowing that if our children have a hardship one day while I am on this earth or not, they can handle all things through Him. Your faithfulness can be the best thing you have ever done for your children and future grandchildren.

Prayer

Lord, I am so proud of my husband. As his wife, I pray my children see in me his integrity. I hope that we together pass down a godly heritage and leave our family a legacy of good things such as having faith and love in God and each other, and they will pass this down to our grandchildren.

I pray each day for my family. I love them with all my heart. I pray for their happiness. I pray that God will always take care of them and lead, guide, and direct them in His footsteps. Amen.

If things are not happening in your timing the way you want, just keep doing your best. God is still in control. We need to leave a legacy to our children and grandchildren. God will bless them through us for future generations to come.

Great Great Grandfather Thomas E. Tart

My great-great grandfather Thomas Eldridge Tart was a Methodist preacher in 1913. He was very proud of his church and members.

My husband's parents were Christians also. That is also why my husband is the man he is today. They had him in church growing up. They taught him Christian ethics. They taught him how to work and be responsible. My mother-in-law was a strong lady. She was an inspiration to our whole family. She always put God first and then family. She has always been here for us. During my cancer, she took care of me by cooking meals and being there. I will always remember her gratitude and loyalty to me in my hard and easy times. Thank you, God, for our Christian heritage.

Both of our children are wonderful, whom my husband and I are so proud of. As of today, they have married wonderful spouses and have wonderful children. They are raising their children—my grandchildren—to know the Lord. There is no greater gift in this world than for parents to do this, and I'm so proud of them.

I hope and pray to God that I have set an example for my children through my years and that I have inspired them. I pray to God that they gained knowledge and strength from my experiences. If any of them are faced with the same diagnoses, I pray that they benefit from my experience.

In Proverbs 13:22, it says, "The measure of a man's character is not what he gets from his ancestors, but what he leaves his descendants." A praying parent is the best thing you can give a child. By reading this book, I hope as the years roll by, God will use my testimonies to show my children, grandchildren, or whoever reads this book the importance of devotion to Christ. I hope and pray that if any of them are tempted to turn away from the will of God, they will be drawn back by the remembrance of my life and testimony.

Be positive. One day, people in your family line will look back and say, "It was because of this man," or "It was because of this woman." If you have godly parents, godly grandparents, you should be extremely grateful. You have more of God's favor and blessings because of what they have done. They paid the price to invest in your future. Great things will happen to you, and doors will open. It will not be just luck; it's because your grandmother was praying. Your parents lived lives marked by excellence, or your great grandparents sowed seeds of integrity. The Bible says when we have this heritage of faith, we will be blessed from it. I thank God every day for my parents and grandparents and for my heritage.

> Dear Lord, help me to know others may be looking at me as a model of faith. Lead, guide, and direct me to know my actions may be examples of what is good. Thank you Jesus for giving me a husband that has always been here for our children and me. Life has had its ups and downs, but I have always had my good Lord to get me through them along with the support of my family. They are always here for me. Amen.

Even though I might have passed and in heaven then, I will still be speaking to them. I want them to know that who we are in Christ enables us to accept what happens in our lives as part of His plan. Once we are convinced that God loves us, we are ready to trust His will for our lives. Trust in God's healing, timing, and His plan. Grow closer to Him. Always know you have someone to lean on, to talk to, and to trust and that He is always with them in their life's journey. I want them to have a spiritual life, enjoy life, have joy and peace in life, and believe in Him and learn through Him. I want them to be happy and laugh a lot and always guard their mind and watch their mouth. Stay positive with faith and read the Bible and know that it is God's Word, and it is the truth. I want them to ask for forgiveness every day for their sins. Know that Jesus died on the cross to save us from our sins. Have faith in Him.

Here is the prayer my grandmother Alice Tart Raynor wrote in 1926 just before my mother, Alice Berneice Raynor, was born.

> I thank thee, Oh Lord, this afternoon, for the opportunity of seeing another day pass this side of eternity. I thank thee for the health and

strength that I enjoy each day. Oh Lord, help to do thy will in spite of the devil and all his works. Let me be thy humble servant.

Lord, give me grace each day to overcome the temptations that I meet in this old world; help me to think of thee and forget the sinfulness of this world. Grant it, Oh Lord, that when this life is finished, my work on earth is done, I may join the angels where I can praise thee forever and ever, and no more sin and sorrow can I see.

My grandmother Alice Tart Raynor passed right after she wrote this giving birth to my mother. My mother had this prayer framed and has it today on her dresser. She is so proud that she had a Christian mother even though she did not get to meet her. My grandmother carried her legacy on with this prayer.

Today, I see the prayer in my mom's house and know my heritage was of great faith. Mom also has a picture of my great granddaddy on her dresser. It is a picture of his church family all gathered in front of the church. My family is a God-centered family and always has been. I know I am where I am today because of my heritage. My family were Christians and had a close relationship with God, and now I am carrying it on to my children and grandchildren.

Inspired by a single photograph and a lifetime of adoration and love for my mother, which is Morgan's grandmother, Alice Berneice Raynor Carlisle. Born October 20, 1926 in Franklinton, North Carolina. My niece Morgan Maris Murphy wrote this little poem in 2012 in memory of my grandmother and her great grandmother, Alice Tart Raynor (1911–1926).

Alice Was Her Name

The picture I have of her is black and white with tattered corners, faded from all the years it's been toted around. Or from the sweet caress of those who loved her and lost.

"Alice was her name"

She looks so young. I wonder what she liked to do for fun. Wearing bobbed hair under a black cloche hat, a standard of the late twenties. Her pale skin a porcelain silhouette.

"Alice was her name"

Such a pretty name. I wonder if she knows I like hats too.

"Alice was her name"

She fell in love like young girls do. Head over heels but her parents disapproved. So, she ran away from home and left her loved ones behind. She got married and was pregnant within no time.

"Alice was her name"

I wonder what she was like. The months went by until it was time. The baby was coming.

Her parents stood by her side. The doctor looked up with his sad eyes and said there is nothing to be done. She is going to die. She was a fighter indeed. She put up a fight. Organs failing and her mother wailing, she had her baby that very night. A beautiful baby girl wrapped in white enters this world as her mother flights.

"Alice was her name" They named the baby Alice, which was my mom and Morgan's grandmother (Born October 20, 1926).

Morgan was so inspired by her grandmother's picture, she wrote this poem. That is carrying a legacy down from generation to generation. I'm so proud of her.

When we read the words of the Bible and grasp the love for Christ that the heroes of the Christian faith left for us, we gain courage to follow their example and to stand strong for those who come after us.

God has a plan for our life and a purpose for our future. No matter what we've been through or what's been done to us, we are still breathing, and God hasn't finished with us yet!

> Thank You, God, for Your healing power. I praise You for the many times You have comforted me. Thank You for watching over me and protecting me. Amen.

"For the word of the Lord is upright, And all His work is done in faithfulness" (Psalm 33:4). The greatest gift we can tie to others is a prayer, so pray for others and yourself. Ask Him for help, and He will be there for you. By prayer, we can leave the future of our world and our loved ones in His hands. God is in control.

Below is a picture of Alice Tart Raynor, my grandmother. Alice was her name.

Alice Tart Raynor (1911–1926)

Chapter 1

GOD'S PERFECT HEALING

Back in the 1970s, my children were so young, and I was having lots of kidney problems, constantly in and out of the doctor's office. I even got pyelonephritis while at work. Pyelonephritis is an inflammation of the kidney and pelvis caused by a bacterial infection. I was in so much pain, they had to call 911 and put me on a stretcher and take me to the hospital. The doctor said my right kidney was in terrible condition, and my left kidney was inflamed. I was so scared. My thoughts were that when I get older, I would probably always have to deal with kidney issues. They gave me antibodies and kept me in the hospital five days. I got better, and they let me go home.

A week after I got out of the hospital, I was at work on a Saturday. I was working overtime. I started having serious pain again in my kidney. I called my mother and said, "Mama, I'm starting to have the same feeling I did before with the pain in my kidneys."

She said, "Brenda, you need to get on your knees and pray. He is the only one that can help you now. The doctors do not seem to help, so go to the Lord."

I got on my knees that day at work, and I prayed from my heart. "Dear Lord, please intervene in my body and rid me of this kidney problem."

I prayed and prayed from my heart. All of a sudden, I felt this whelm go over me. I could tell the Lord answered my prayer. My pain went away as of that moment. I went to the doctor a week later for my checkup of the hospital stay. The doctor could not believe his eyes. He said my right and left kidney were in perfect condition. Nothing was wrong with them.

Before this miracle of healing, I had constantly been back and forth to the doctor with infections for over a year. The doctor had even told me my right kidney was at a stage of not working. Now after my prayer for a healing, the doctors could not believe their eyes. It was a miracle that my kidneys were perfect. As of today, thirty years later, I have not had any kidney infections or problems with my kidneys. Thank you, Jesus. You did it. You did a miracle on me. It was His Healing that healed me. Thank you, Jesus.

God wants to heal you. You have to be persuaded that God wants to heal you. Do not have doubt in your mind. As long as there is doubt in your mind, perfect faith cannot exist, and until you have perfect faith, without doubt or wavering, you may never be healed.

Our faith is always being tested, especially on our most challenging days. We live in a fallen world, but God works in the midst of this. His presence is there for those who open their eyes to see it, and He brings good out of the situation. Do not be angry or doubt God.

God is our great healer. The doctors are smart and hardworking. They have relieved my suffering on many occasions, and I am grateful for their intelligence in diagnosing illnesses and prescribing medication. God appointed humans to have knowledge to help take care of us. God created us with the ability to heal. Doctor's would be useless if He had not created us this way. I believe no healing takes place apart from God, but this does not mean that I place my faith in doctors rather than God.

Without faith, it is impossible to please Him; for they that come to God must believe that He is, and that He is a rewarder of them that diligently seek Him. (Hebrews 11:6)

But let them ask in faith, nothing wavering. For they that waver are like a wave of the sea with the wind and tossed. For let not those (who waver) think they shall receive anything of the Lord. (James 1:6–7)

You need to be convinced that God wants to heal you and that it is not God's will for you to be sick. After being convinced, you will always receive healing when prayed for if not before. You also need to have faith, which is confidence that God will keep His promise to you.

Chapter 2

GOD'S PERFECT TIMING

In the 1990s, my back was hurting constantly. I could not sit, stand, walk, or ride in a car. I could not get out of a chair or off of a couch without crucial pain. I had pain radiating through my right leg. I went to a neurologist (nerve doctor). The doctor did not x-ray me. He said to me, "You are getting older, and you have to expect this."

I could picture myself in a wheel chair soon. He just told me to take a pain reliever and get rest. That was not what I wanted to hear. That I had to just live with this pain and medicate the problem. He even said it might get worse. I went away from the doctor's office in tears.

That night, I started to bed. I got on my knees beside the bed, and I prayed from my heart to the Lord to help me. I knew He had answered my prayer for my kidney problems and healed me so "He" can this time also. I prayed so hard and cried and begged the good Lord to please heal my back. I then felt the whelm go over me just like before when He healed my kidneys. I knew then He had healed me. I was so happy. I got straight up from my knees and went to bed.

The next morning, I woke up and my back was hurting so bad. I said, "Lord, I felt the whelm go over me. I know You heard my prayer. I felt Your whelm go over me. Why am I hurting?"

At that time, I took a shower and let warm water run on my back to help the pain. I went on doing my daily chores, which was so hard to do because of the pain. That afternoon, I went to Kmart. I bought three potted plants. I rolled the three plants in a cart to the trunk of my car, and I was thinking, *Lord, help me be able to lift these plants up to put them in my car.*

As I started to the car, this old man with a beautiful smile came up to me and said, "Madam, you look like you are in pain. Can I help you?"

I said, "Yes, thank you."

He had the prettiest smile on his face, and it just glowed. He said, "What doctor are you going to?"

I said, "I am going to a neurologist."

He said, "You don't need to go to a neurologist. You need to go to an orthopedic [bone doctor]."

I said, "But I have pain going down my leg along with the back pain."

He said, "You still need to go to an orthopedic doctor and apply some miracle gel on your back.

While he was standing there talking to me, I found a piece of paper in the car and wrote on it, "Go to an orthopedic doctor and rub miracle gel on my back." I thanked him for helping me with the pots and his information. He then went on his way.

The next day, I got out my phone book and looked up orthopedic doctor. The first one I came to I called and made an appointment with him. He saw me that day. The first thing he did was take an X-ray of my spine. I was so scared. I could just see him showing me the X-ray, and it would be with in a serious condition.

After the X-ray, the doctor came in and put the X-ray up on a light in the room I was in. He said, "Look at this. You have a spine of a young person. It is perfect. It looks great. Your back is not strong because you don't exercise. Your muscles are weak, which makes your tendons sore when you exert yourself. You just need to take a muscle relaxer and use the miracle gel, and you will be fine."

I went home and did what he said, and in two weeks I could run, swim, walk, drive, do anything. My back was healed. It was healed in "His" timing, not mine. The lesson I learned from this is that the Lord did answer my prayer when I prayed so hard that night.

He answered it in His timing and not mine. I should have never questioned Him. I did not even realize when the old man came up to me that he was part of God's plan to heal me. He sent the angel—the old man—to tell me what to do. How many times does someone just come up to you and say, "What doctor do you go to?" It was of the Lord.

I went back to Kmart, and I looked for the old man out in the garden area. I could not find him. I asked a lady there in the garden area if she knew the man. I described him, and she did not know who I was talking about. I then realized he was an angel. The Lord sent him to me to tell me what to do to be healed. The Lord let me know what I had to do to get healed.

Thank you, Jesus. You healed me again. You healed me in your timing. Forgive me for being so ignorant as to question you about your healing. Thank you for the old man (the angel) giving me the information I needed. Thank you, Jesus.

The Lord will answer our prayers in His timing, by His method, according to His purposes. We can trust Him. After we pray, our response we can make for healing is to praise God for His answer and to leave all the details of His answer up to Him. The way God gets us through a difficult time is often a step-by-step process, decision by decision, steady obedience. This is His way! God's timing is always perfect.

We pray and ask God to hurry up and bless what we want. God says, "Be patient and wait upon me." We can trust His response, even if it doesn't come in the time we expect. It could be God's way of protecting us. It can be the start of something better than we could imagine. When you walk with God, He will take care of you. Don't be impatient. It's not over until God says it's over. Sometimes God works fast, but other times, He works slow and gradual, requiring steady obedience on our part and in His timing. The Lord will answer our prayers by His method and His purpose. We can trust Him.

Trust in God. Don't let your emotions control you like mine did. Wait on God. He will help strengthen you. Allow His strength and healing power to work on you. God promises to take care and watch over us. He will not leave us.

When we pray, we always think it should happen now. I was wanting it to happen in my timing. I wanted it to happen as soon as I prayed, but I needed to wait for His timing. Don't do like I did. I questioned Him, which I should never do. You need to talk to Him and tell Him you know He is working on your behalf, and you will have patience and wait for His timing. If you wait for Him, you will see His wonderful works, working for your good. God is never in a hurry, but He is always on time.

It may seem that we take one step backward for every two steps forward, but if we could see the bigger picture of what God is doing, we could conclude "things are getting better." We just need to wait on Him and trust Him.

In our lives, we find ourselves waiting for things to change, for something to happen, for more money, for the right door to open, for life to get back to normal, for your relationship to get better. We want action fast and in our timing. Have trust that the Lord will help you by showing you the right pathway. Put your life in God's hand with faith. God has a timetable. Just be patient and wait for Him to accomplish it His way and His time. Just be positive and trust Him because He is the one and only one in control of our future.

In life, there will be obstacles. Don't worry; stay in God's Word and pray. Do not doubt yourself. Have faith in yourself, and you will have a dream, goal, and hope.

You are God's child. I know I love my children and grandchildren, and He loves you the same. He will not forget to complete the work that He has begun. God has a master plan in His timing designed for us, and He will accomplish it. Joy and peace are found in believing God has a purpose and plan for us. When you have a gift of faith, things seem easier, but to someone else without that gift of faith, they may seem impossible. Your future can be brighter than your past. Be faithful because in the right time and way, He will move.

Trusting God always requires patience. God does not work on our timetable. Patience lets us enjoy life while we trust Him by waiting. Trusting God in His timing is the best option.

Those who wait on the Lord shall renew their strength to motivate and find their strength in Him. When we are tired of trying to handle our issues ourselves and become frustrated in our efforts, we need to wait on the Lord to get us through it. We do this by spending time with him, meditating on His Word, worshipping Him, and keeping Him in our life and thoughts constantly. Have a relationship with Him by praying and talking to Him. Go to Him with everything. Tell Him your problems. By doing this, we become more like Him. This will calm you through the hard times of your life with a sense of peace knowing that the Lord is with you and that all is well.

I heard this story one time that when a train goes through a tunnel and it gets dark, you don't jump off. You sit still and put trust in the engineer. We need to trust God no matter how dark our situation is. God says, "You are coming out."

- Matthew 25:21 says that when you are faithful in the little things, will give you greater things when you remain faithful. God rewards those who seek after Him.
- Ephesian 2:10 says, "You are God's masterpiece." God puts us in situations that forces us to use our faith. We may be uncomfortable, but God knows what He is doing. God is in control. You may get disappointed, but learn to lean on Him. He takes care of us.
- Be patient and know God will do it in his timing, not yours. God never takes anything from His children unless He gives us something better (Luke 11:10–13).
- Waiting is difficult but it serves a vital purpose. It means making a decision to trust and obey God even when things are not going the way you planned (Hebrews 6:15).
- Just because it hasn't happened yet doesn't mean God has changed His mind. While you are waiting, God is working (James 1:4).
- "Be still in the Lord and wait patiently for Him" (Psalm 37:7). We need to wait for God. He teaches us to trust Him. His timing is not our timing. God may not do things

the way we want Him to, but He will always act according to His timing.

- "Lead me in Your truth and teach me, For You are the God of my salvation; for You I wait all the day" (Psalm 25:5).

The best response we can make after our prayers for healing is to praise God for His answers and to leave all the details of His answer to Him.

Chapter 3

GOD'S PERFECT PLAN
(YEAR 2008/2009)

Before my cancer, my life was as good as good could be. I was on the top of the world. My husband, children, and family were in good health. For the first time, my children were having my grandchildren. I had just retired. I could sleep in late. My husband's job was doing great. I didn't have to work. I was, as they say, "on cloud nine." We were in the process of building our dream retirement home on the lake. We had our house plans and a builder to start the project ready to go. Life was so good.

I had a strong relationship with the Lord. In my mind, the Lord will always take care of me. I will never have cancer or anything. The Lord will never let such a thing happen to me. I prayed constantly, "Lord, take care of me and my family"

Then all of a sudden, my whole world changed in one day, the day I was diagnosed with cancer. "No, this can't be! Not me, not cancer. I might die. Not now, not me."

Below is my story of when I was diagnosed: "God's Perfect Plan with My Cancer Story."

November 2008 is when I was diagnosed with cancer. In 2006 through 2008, I had told the doctor I had been hurting in my joints and back, and my thumbnail was thicker. He told me that it's because of my age, and I had arthritis. He kept me on pain medicine to relieve my joint and back pain. I was not coughing or having any lung issues.

Now in 2008, I went to the doctor with a pain in the right side of my chest. The doctor said I had an infection. He put me on an antibiotic for seven days. I took the antibiotic seven days, and I was still hurting in my chest. I called the doctor on Friday. He wanted me to come in on the following Monday for an appointment, and he will give me another antibiotic if necessary. So at that time, I made an appointment with him for the following Monday.

On Saturday morning, the next day, I packed my car to go to my parents' house. I had them food in the cooler, and my dog was in my car. My dog's name is Abby. She is a red cocker spaniel, whom I love very much. She is my baby.

As I started down the highway, I had a pain to shoot down my right arm to my right middle finger. The first thought I got was could this be a heart attack? No, because it is in my right arm, not my left. But then I remembered women can have it to attack in their neck, back, etc. So why not in my right arm.

I am the type of person that procrastinates. I usually would have said, "I'll wait till tomorrow or I have an appointment on Monday. I'll wait till then." But instead, my car went off the exit and headed back to my house. It's like the exit was there, and I steered off not even thinking twice about it. It was the Lord!

I got home, let my dog out, got the food out of the cooler, and put it in the refrigerator. I headed straight to the urgent care. I called my husband on the way. He left work immediately and came to the urgent care and met me there. The doctor right away x-rayed my chest and gave me an EKG. He came in and said, "The X-ray of your chest looks great, and the EKG looks great. We don't have a lot of high tech equipment here. If you want to go to the emergency room at the hospital, they can check you further. They have more equipment there."

I asked him for a prescription for another antibiotic for the infection so that I will not have to go to the appointment on Monday. He gave it to me. I told my husband, Gary, to take me home. "I will be fine. I have the antibiotic for my infection in my chest that probably caused the pain in my arm. I will take it, and if I'm not better by Monday, I will go to the doctor then."

He took me home, and he went back to work. My daughter Lisa called me and said, "Mama, I don't feel good about this. You could have a heart attack tonight."

I told her the same thing I told my husband. "I'll be okay. I'm going to take this prescription of antibiotics."

She got off the phone and called her daddy, and the next thing I knew, Gary was standing in the kitchen saying, "Get in the car because we are going to the emergency room."

He was so persistent and demanding. I thought, *We'll, if it's that important to them, then okay.*

We got to the emergency room, and the doctor gave me another EKG. They did blood work and said they are going to give me a CAT scan. I asked, "Why a CAT scan when I'm here for a heart attack?"

They answered, "We have to see how your blood in your arteries are flowing to your heart."

I said, "Okay."

The doctor came out later and said, "Yes, you do have an infection in your chest, and you do need to take the antibiotic, but we have bad news. We found a tumor in your right lung. You need to get an appointment with a lung specialist." *Cancer?*

I could hardly bring myself to say the word. I thought in my mind, *What, a tumor in my lung? Why? Could it be scar tissue or could it be cancer.*

Numbly, I stumbled out of the doctor's office. My mind was in a fog. My husband was just as numb as I was. We walked down the hall to the insurance office. The lady there was setting me up an appointment with a lung specialist.

As I sat there, I could feel my eyes filling up with tears. As I looked up at my husband, his eyes were filling up with tears. We were both in shock and in disbelief. My husband went to the restroom next to the office where we were at, and I knew he was crying.

The doctor walked by, and he looked at me as if he felt so sorry for me. That was the first time I felt so helpless. I have always felt invulnerable. Cancer was something that happened to other people.

But instead, it happened to me. I can't believe I have cancer in my body, the body that has always been so good to me. I could not even say the word cancer.

I started praying. "Oh Lord, please not me. Please, help me."

After a couple of minutes, I pulled myself together, dried my eyes. My husband and I walked out to the car, and we could not speak. We were both in shock and scared. I called my children and told them, and we were all in shock. "God, dear God," I sobbed, "please give me a miracle. Please don't let me have cancer. Let this be benign. This can't happen to me. I've always tried to be careful and take care of myself. I've never smoked. Why me, dear Lord? Why me? Not me. Dear Lord, not me."

My husband looked at me and said, "Honey, don't worry. It's probably benign. It could be scare tissue or something else, not cancer."

"God, please don't let it be cancer."

When we got home, my husband got on the telephone and called a close friend that had cancer in the past and is a cancer survivor. The wonderful friend called the doctor for us, and the doctor called us. The doctor said, "Be in my office tomorrow morning."

The oncologist had a whole team ready for me. I've never seen anything happen so fast. Within a couple of days, I was in the hospital getting a biopsy. I had to get a biopsy of my lung to see if I had cancer.

What was so amazing about this situation is that when I first entered the radiation room where they did the biopsy, I saw the doctor's assistant and thought she was an unpleasant person. I guess I was so scared, I noticed every little thing. I just wanted help and hope. She did not even have a smile on her face. She even looked unhappy. I smiled at her, and she didn't smile back, and then when the doctor started the procedure, she came up and took my hand and rubbed my arm.

As the doctor was putting the needle straight in through my chest to go into my lung, she said the sweetest words to me. She said, "The Lord is taking care of you."

It meant so much to me. She held my hand and was so sweet. She had a smile on her face. She said, "You are going to be fine. The Lord is telling me now. I work with lung patients, and in my heart you, will be fine. I just know it. You will witness one day to others with cancer. You will be a survivor."

When she told me that, I was so happy. It was like an angel was talking to me from the Lord. I had a ray of hope at that very moment. I needed it so bad. I was constantly wanting just a pinch of hope. I felt the Lord was talking through her to me. She was another angel that God sent to give me hope. What I am saying is that you can have someone to come to you and relay to you what the Lord is wanting you to hear. That person is an angel carrier.

The Lord relays His messages to us in different ways. Take note of each and every one. At that time, I had no hope when I walked into that radiation room to have my biopsy. I felt so heavy with fear. For her to say that, it meant so much to me. At a time like this, you need all comforting words possible. I really believe she was an angel of God's telling me this. I told Gary, my husband, the minute I got out of the radiation room what she said, and he said, "Brenda, that was the Lord."

Never will I leave you, nor forsake you.
(Hebrews 13:5)

I had to set up a biopsy and CAT scan. The biopsy will show if it is cancer and what kind it is. I then had to get a PET scan of my lung to show if it had spread. My husband requested that they tell him so he could give me the good or bad news.

A couple of days later, after taking the PET scan, my husband came home with the news. He walked in the bedroom where I was, and I could see the answer on his face. He hugged me and started crying, telling me that I do have cancer in my right lung and that my lymph nodes in my baronial area also are cancerous. We both cried and prayed. "This can't be happening to me," I cried.

That was the beginning of the long journey with cancer. A journey I never thought I would take.

We all have a plan for our lives that is built on our dreams. Our plans can change into prayers. Sometimes we lose hope. The things you think you needed are not important anymore and the things you didn't think you needed you can do without.

"Father, my whole world is falling apart. How can this be happening to me? I don't understand what is happening. Lord, help me to see this is all part of your plan to give me a future with hope. God I ask for a healing. Amen"

I always for some reason thought I would live a long life. My parents are in their eighties and nineties and still living. I'm only sixty. I'm too young to die. I have new grandchildren. I have just got where I can stay home and not work full-time.

I have a wonderful husband whom I don't want to let go of. I have lots of friends. I want to see my children and grandchildren grow up. I don't want to die and hurt my mama, daddy and my loved ones. We just bought a beach house, and I love going there. We are in the process of building a new home on the lake. Gary, and I have so many plans and goals ahead. Gary, and I are just starting to enjoy each other because our children are grown, and we have more time for ourselves.

Prayer

Oh, dear Lord, not now, not me. I love life, dear Lord. Please don't let me die. We are only human beings. We can only see the present and the past. The future is always frightening to us.

Lord, this is a scary journey to make, a journey I thought I would never take. I'm all alone and very scared of the unknown. I can hardly cope because all I want is hope. All I see is that this just can't be happening to me. I can't sleep at night, and I can't even fight.

I know You will do me right and show me an angel in sight. I need You God to lead me to succeed, which I know You can indeed.

My oncologist started setting me up appointments with my surgeon and radiologist. My oncologist said I had stage 3A lung cancer, adenocarcinoma. He said since it had gone into my esophagus area, I will need chemotherapy, surgery, and radiation. They did an MRI on my brain to see if it had spread there. They told me it came back good with no cancer. "Thank You, Lord. Thank You."

After being diagnosed with cancer, I had all kinds of emotional reactions. All my family and friends were so concerned and wanted me to be okay. I went through a grieving process.

In the period immediately following my active treatment, I found myself searching for my "new normal." Treatments made it difficult to resume my activities as quickly as I wanted to because of my weakness. My immune system was very low. My recovery seemed to be slow. I started changing my daily routine. My body changed in so many ways, and I had to be patient for my immune system to build up to normal. I found that I was scared and frightened. The doctors had done all they could do. I now was on my own. I was confused about my future.

The initial shock of this was disbelief. I experienced sadness and depression with my anxiety. I had so many feelings to go through me. I felt angry, anxiety, depression, fear, disappointed, deceived, threatened, guilt, bitter, hopelessness, self-pity, irritable, lack of confidence, loneliness, scared, ugly, worried, suffering, emotional, manipulated, betrayed, mistreated, defensive, and helpless.

Cancer gave me a negative attitude and negative emotions, which was fear that I'm losing control over my body and my life. I then had anger because this is happening. Then I had depression over what I endured. These are all normal feelings. I had anxiety by feeling jittery. Anxiety steals our joy. My stomach was tied in knots. My mouth was dry. My appetite disappeared. I felt like my nerve endings were frazzled. I felt like my body was in a constant state of electric shock. I had sweaty palms and a fluttery heart. I had insomnia, restlessness, early awaking, irritability, loss of appetite, fatigue, inability to concentrate, an absence of interest in activities. I dreaded to get up in the morning.

These questions also naturally came into my mind:

- What do people think of me now?
- Will people always look at me as a cancer survivor instead of Brenda?
- Will I get my life back again?
- Will I be able to cope emotionally and physically with this?
- Should I clean out my closets so my children will not have to do it?
- Will I ever have a normal life again?
- Will my hair come back?
- How long do I have to live?
- How long will I be with my grandchildren and children?
- Will my parents at their age be able to cope with this?
- What job can I do now?
- Will I be able to work again?
- Should I set goals?
- Am I putting too much pain on my children, husband, and family to go through this?
- Will I ever feel like me (Brenda) again?
- Will I always be a cancer victim?
- Why, God? Why have You let this happen to me? I've always tried to be healthy, Lord. Why me?
- God, what are You telling me?
- Could this disease have been avoided?
- Is this Your plan for my life?
- Lord, is this from the devil?
- Have I done anything to cause this?
- Lord, are You putting me to the test?
- Is this a death sentence?

It is so hard to understand why bad things happen to good people, but we need to understand that nothing seems to make sense when a disease strikes you like this. When something like this happens, you are helpless, something you are not in control of. You keep thinking, *Why did this happen to me?* You draw into a shell of denial and depression, hoping you will not get worse.

Fear and uncertainty about the end of my life caused me anxiety. I started working long hours. I started all kinds of activities. I felt fear, which is a major cause of stress. The more I feared, the more anxiety I had. Fear drives us away from people and responsibility. It can be self-protecting, or it can be self-destructive. I felt self-pity, which is an expression of anger toward God. It causes depression. Every night, I went to bed thinking. Every morning, I awoke thinking that I couldn't believe I have cancer. I was so scared of the treatments ahead. Every day as I got ready for the day, I wondered in the back of my mind what would happen if I don't get better and would die.

I wanted to clean up my house so I could stay busy and not think. I wanted to see the cup half full and not half empty. I wanted someone to say, "Brenda, you are going to be okay." I wanted reassurance that I'm going to live. I wanted a cure. I didn't want cancer.

Then I started feeling guilt about causing my cancer. Was it secondhand smoke? Was it the chemicals I worked with? Was it radon? What did I do to cause this? I couldn't do anything but think, *Why me? What did I do.* I wanted an answer to why my cancer developed.

My diagnoses were devastating. I have laughed, cried, yelled in anger. I have been frustrated. I worried, and I was concerned. I felt isolated from the "healthy world." I wondered if anyone understood. I craved success stories. I felt helpless. I had questions: "Why me?" I lost my hair, my eye lashes, my eyebrows. I felt as if I were being erased. I felt a less a person than I did before. I was so fatigued, pale, and sick.

When I ask the doctor about my prognosis, he gave me no incentive of being cured. If anything, he made me feel worse. I would look in the computer for just something that would make me feel better, but it made me feel anxiety. The doctors never told me anything encouraging. I was so confused.

Cancer is fought on three battlefields: your mind, your heart, and your body. Your mind screams, and your heart cries. It is so hard to believe that my body has this disease in it. I was so weak and sad. I didn't feel like Brenda. I wanted to feel happy and be Brenda again.

My sadness made me depressed. Perhaps it was knowing I had a terrible disease. I would wake up each morning wanting to think positive and be happy. It never worked. A cloud of despair would go over me and smother any positive thoughts I had. I had a lack of interest in life. The heavy clouds did not want to leave me. I could either give in to this depression and die, or I can fight. I didn't have any strength left in me to fight. I started to praying and asking the Lord to please be with me. I wanted a positive attitude and not a negative attitude.

I always seem to have had an easy life. My mind always told me that it was because of my strength. But when trouble hits, I realized how little strength I have and how helpless I am.

God blesses us with success and peace. But when the enemy attacks, we then realize how powerless we are without God's help. All I can say is, if you have ever been in the place of "no hope," until you are there, you will never know how much you need God.

The doctors told me I have had cancer for three years. I then remembered my pains in my back and joints for the last three years were so intense. I had no idea what was ahead. I couldn't believe I had not found this sooner.

I went to my primary care doctor, and she put me on an antidepressant for a short period to help me get through this. I needed this antidepressant because I caught myself wanting to sit around the house, lying in the bed a lot of the day, and having thoughts constantly of dying. How to handle life's problems can be difficult. I have faith, but I was scared. I felt that I needed this medicine to take the edge off.

There are questions that we all seem to ask when something like this invades our comfort zone. The first questions we ask: "Why, God?" "Why me?" "Why am I the one who must suffer this pain?"

God knows this is a natural response. It does not mean I am doubting God, but I am seeking understanding. God is not upset with me. He knows everything about me from the beginning, and He is not surprised or disappointed about my confusion. He knows I might become angry and say, "God, if You really loved me, You would not do this to me!"

God may or may not give me an answer. It may not have been God. What I need to remember is that God allows Satan in his wicked attacks into our experience. But the devil (Satan) cannot go beyond God's divine boundary. The battle of cancer is fought in both physically and spiritually. Fear, anxiety, depression, loneliness, and despair are at us constantly. The enemy wants us to think that we have cancer because we've done something wrong. Our protection from these attacks is faith. Remember God's unconditional love for you and use it as a shield to protect you physically and spiritually.

Even unbelievers will cry, "God, help me!" when faced with a crisis. God, what are you trying to tell me? Could it had been avoided? What causes this? Is this part of Your plan for my life? There was no way I could head off on my own and have handled this. I had to look up into the face of God, take His hand, and say, "Lord, lead me in the path You have for me. I want to walk with You.

Four months later, while going through chemo, my husband's business went down. "Oh no! My health and now my husband's business." My dream house was just a dream that I had to put on hold, and then my daddy died that same year. What more can happen to me? My dreams seemed to be over, and it looked like this situation was permanent. All the facts show it is over. I couldn't see how I could ever rise any higher out of this situation. All the facts were telling me and my husband that's it's impossible to get out of this terrible situation.

My dreams and goals seemed to have been gone in just a few days. I wanted to be healthy again and my husband's business to be operable. Everyone has always said cancer is a death sentence. A miracle had to happen. By the cars not being made, my husband was not going to have a job, which meant no money to be made to live. We had doctor bills and payment to be made. What are we going to do?

My dad died during my surgery recovery, and I couldn't even go to his funeral. My world seemed to be turning upside down. I started praying, "Lord, please get us through this. Help me to grow stronger in my faith." I had to turn my crises over to the Lord and let Him handle this because I couldn't.

At this time, I knew my anxiety can only change through my faith in God. Others can encourage, help, and support us, but it's up to us to handle this problem the right way. And I knew that God will guide me through this. With God beside me, we can conquer this cancer. A crisis breaks the normal pattern of life. During this crisis, I was in shock! It may lead to growth or disaster. It will bring about a major turning point in my life for good or bad. I know I cannot control the crisis that comes into my life, but I can control my reactions to these crises. Dealing with a crisis will make me face something in my life that I would rather not deal with. I need to let Go and let God.

For most of us, cancer wasn't part of our plans. We didn't chose to go through countless test and wait anxiously for the results, or take weeks out of our life for surgery or treatment regimens. However, we can stop cancer from taking over our spirit by choosing to put our hope in the Lord. He has plans for our life. God's plan for our lives may not be our dreams. His plan may be something we never imagined. We can trust Him to work out those plans. He will stay with us through everything we face, no matter what.

Chapter 4

TURNED MY CRISES OVER TO THE LORD

As a human, I was scared. I knew I had to face reality. I could not believe this happened to me, but it did happen to me, so I need to go forward for a chance of recovery. I need to take responsibility. I need to take action to deal with this situation. I knew God is the only one in control of it.

You may ask, "Why, God, did You do this to me in the first place? Do You no longer love me? Why me, Lord? Did I do something wrong in Your eyes?" I've always tried to be healthy. Lord, why me? Why not me? I'm no different from anyone else. The Bible says, "There are going to be storms in our life." What we have to do is to fight and come through the storm.

By being depressed, it was as if I am questioning God's control over these circumstances. God made us with the capacity for depression; however, He did not intend it to defeat us but to correct us. You say, "I can't help it. I don't want to feel this way." I know I will not be able to overcome depression by simply wanting, wishing, or praying it away. I know my attitude and actions can make me soar to the heights of happiness or plunge into the depths of despair. I know I can't always control my emotions, and I also know I need to be strong and fight. By fighting, I mean grow stronger in my faith and lean on the Lord for my healing. I need to have faith and positive actions to overcome this. I need to have faith that God will get me through this.

I need to know I have cancer, but cancer does not have me. I am God's child. God will comfort and fight for me. I need to look at cancer as being a beatable, treatable, survivable disease, and I had to be positive and have faith that the Lord is going to take care of me.

I got on my hands and knees and prayed to God. I prayed for healing and guidance. Each night and day, I prayed. I knew the key to handling this problem is learning to trust God with them. I need to commit my problems to God and turn them over to Him so I will grow in His grace and be healed.

Sometimes, life can be rough. It is like a road. Roads are meant to be smooth, but they can get rough. It can lead to excitement and joy, or it can lead to failure and sadness. It is never success without failure or gain without pain. My journey to wellness was scary.

The rougher the road gets, the more you will face the realities of life itself. At this time, you will then have to decide the direction your life will take. Sometimes, there will be others to help you along. But at other times, you will find yourself traveling alone. Just remember, God is with you. He will help you find your answers to all your problems. He will share your heartaches and bear your burdens. No matter what you are facing, God will be there to help you.

I knew that how I handle this problem will be the key to overcoming it. If not, I will remain stuck in my own self-absorbed indecision and inability to solve my problems. I can do it my way, or I can do it His way. My way is impossible. I choose God's way, which is my only hope, my only cure, my only controller of this disease, my everything. I will be totally dependent upon Him for my healing!

God is available to us as a source of courage, strength, and energy. We can choose to wallow in our misery, or we can choose to move forward into joy and peace. Nothing is too good for you to receive as a believer in Jesus. God does not desire for us to be sick. He desires that we experience His very best of healing and blessings.

So often, it's easy to get disappointed, get negative, and start thinking that it will not happen. But just because I didn't see anything happening fast did not mean God is not working. My mind could have started thinking, *It's over. It's impossible.*

I had to change my way of thinking. I need to think positive. I knew I had to do my part and believe even though it looked impossible. I knew it may not happen the way I expected it to or on my timetable, but God is faithful, and He will not let me down. I need to trust in Him. He will then give me strength through my battle. He will give me wisdom with my decisions, and then I will receive peace knowing He is with me. God wants for us to have hope in Him. He wants us to recall who He is and what He has done. And when we do, no disappointment can keep us from hope. If you look carefully, you'll discover that God is working in your life every day. God answers prayers. Ask God to help you see His love for you.

Psalm 16. I know the Lord is always with me. I will not be shaken, for He is right beside me.

No wonder my heart is filled with joy, and my mouth shouts with praises! You have to have the desire to fight back. It is difficult to fight, but if you go on the offensive from day 1, you have a much greater chance of survival than those who are fearful. I realized I need to take control of this illness. I need to read and ask questions, search for knowledge. I need to live in the present one day at a time. Life is a precious gift from God. I needed to talk to Him and grow closer to Him.

God wants me to draw closer to Him and not see it as the termination of my future. He does not want me to be angry. He does not want me to lose patience at this time. He wants me to grow in faith.

Do we trust Him to provide, or do we get angry and take it out on others? Do we understand that God is testing us in order to prepare us for what He is going to do in or lives, or do we believe He is forsaking us? The answer we give to these questions are the keys to passing the test. He wants to bless us in so many ways, and He can't unless we are completely submitted to Him.

As I went to the doctor; they never gave me hope, but God did. You may never find what or who caused the cancer. God comforts us in our troubles and not necessarily that He removes us from our trouble, but we need to understand that this can be a renewing experience with God. God can use this as a blessing in your life if you trust Him for the outcome.

The key to handling my problem was to learn to trust what God tells me to do about it, and then I need to do it with the confidence that He will bless it. I knew that if I obey God's commands, He will bless me. I trusted His love in spite of this terrible circumstance. No matter how bad this crisis may appear to be, it is never beyond His abilities to resolve it.

One of the most frustrating aspects of the cancer experience is the way it takes over our daily routine. The mound of unfinished projects and obligations becomes enormous. Focusing on these things only makes us more anxious. Peace comes when we focus on God's presence even when things are undone. He promised to meet our needs, to protect us, and to never leave us. Peace doesn't come when we figure out how to get everything done. It only comes when we focus on what He's already done. You need to get God's prospective on your problem.

When I got my diagnoses, Jesus was with me. I could feel Him with me and His angels with me. When I went into surgery and had radiation, He was with me. Christ is living in me. He will never leave me alone.

When I was diagnosed with cancer, I knew it was going to be a difficult battle. I turned to my Lord and Savior for my healing. I turned to my family and friends for support, and I relied on my team of doctors to provide care. I was confident that I was going to defeat this disease with the Lord's help. I knew that my job was to fight back with medical treatment while nurturing my mind and spirit with faith that the Lord will take care of me. He helped me find it, and He will help me get rid of it. I worked at trying to have a positive attitude even though the experience is very traumatic. I prayed every hour during that time.

One night, as I was praying, I stopped and listened, and God spoke to me and said, "I have blessings coming your way. I will be with you during all this time. Get ready, I hear your wants through your prayers. I will get you through this health situation. I will change your life back to the way it was before or even better. I have blessings that will help you for years to come to have your life back. Just have faith in Me. Fear not, for I am with you. You need to wait for my timing and for my plan for you."

As I prayed, I could feel myself get closer to the Lord. I prayed from my heart. These are my darkest days. I need Him so much. I now look to God and not myself for my healing. He is the only one that can help me. I have to be positive and hope for the best. I refuse to dwell on my bad health. I will be optimistic through my faith in the Lord. I need to keep up my strength and confidence. I have to take charge of my feelings. It's so hard to deal with emotions mentally at a time like this, but I know I need to beat this cancer with my Lord's help. I feel so many powerful negative emotions. I need to comfort my fears and not magnify them by keeping my head up and seeing the glass half full and not half empty.

My faith has grown since I have gone through some of life's deepest valleys, and I have found that I was never alone. God was always right there beside me. A lot of struggling came from my thinking. Anxiety comes from wondering about things. I let my imagination create the worst possible, and then I gave into fear. He wants us to live in peace and joy and trust Him. I've always heard the opposite of fear is faith.

Ephesians 6:16. In every battle you will need faith. I then felt that I could see a light at the end of the tunnel. I knew I needed to fight this disease through the healing power of my Lord Jesus Christ. I rely on faith for my strength. I constantly pray every day, every hours, every minute. I know to be effective, I have to Pray from my heart and not my mouth. We must be submissive to God. In time of personal crises, we can turn to Him for strength. I began to see light instead of darkness to appear. Life began to be so much more victorious. I know that Satan cannot lay a disease on my body. I will resist Satan and his disease. I do not fear him. I will take a firm stand. I rebuke Satan in the name of Jesus.

When I started realizing the Lord is working with me. I started getting more and more confident that He is in control of this plan, and He is going to cure me. I had hope. He helped me find this so He can get rid of it. Thank you, Jesus. The more the Lord became the focus of my desire and praise, the more my problems seem to disappear. When I put my focus on the Lord and upon Him alone, everything else in my life was a state of calmness, including my problems. The more I glorified God, the smaller my needs and problems became. Faith became stronger, and I knew my heavenly Father will take care of me.

As of then I could feel God with me so strong. You may think you can never rise any higher, especially in a situation like this, but He can do anything. When it does happen, it will be so amazing, you will know it had to be the hand of God. That's what happened to me.

Chapter 5

LET GO, LET GOD

As I went through my hard time with my struggle with my kidneys, back, and cancer, I had to lay down my expectations and put them in the Lord's hand. He is the only one to turn to. He is the only one in control. He is the only one who will never fail me.

I need to live in the present, one day at a time. Life is a precious gift from God. One of my favorite quotes is "Yesterday's the past, tomorrow's the future but, today is a gift. That's why it's called the present" (author unknown).

I need to fight this disease and pray. I need to take His hand and let Him lead me. As my mama keeps reminding me over and over, the Lord helped me find this, and He will get rid of it. He has a plan for me. His hands are in all of this. He healed my kidney's with His healing. He healed my back with His timing, and He will heal my cancer with His plan.

I knew in my heart that God works miracles. I knew He wants us to pray and ask for His miracle. I thought It was too much to ask for, but it's not too much for the Lord. He will answer you back if you stop and listen to Him. He will then give you hope and peace.

I know a person's mind is very powerful. I knew I needed to stay positive, not fear, and I need to have faith and love. I had to be at peace. I needed God to fight the battle for me. The doctors told me, "Brenda, no stress, no worrying. This will make you worse."

I was too weak to fight the battle. Even though I don't like my health situation and very uncomfortable. I knew I had to keep going. I can't give up. I can't sit around and feel sorry for myself. I said, "I'm not going to let this disease take over my life. I'm going to deal with it and move on." I need to Let go, let God. I had to turn to God to help me.

When life's problem lay you flat on your back, the only direction you can look is up. Some of life's problems are so great that only God can solve them. He is the only one that could help me in this crisis. Cancer is something that only He can control. As I grew up as a child, my parents were always there to handle my every need and problem. If I got sick, within twenty-four hours, I was well. When I married, my husband was always there to handle my problems. This was different. All I could do along with my parents and husband is look up and pray, which was what I needed to do. I needed God at this time—only God.

No one ever chooses tragedies like these. We'd much rather have the "good life" of minimum pain. But suffering is a real part of human experience. Suffering is having to put up with something you want to change very much. But you are powerless to make it right. You may never know the reason why you suffer, but you can choose how you respond to suffering.

It's like the farmer that sows and cultivates a garden. We have faith that God will send the sunshine and rain. This is something we cannot do. We must leave the results to God. We need to trust God and have faith by leaving the results for Him to take care of it. If you have a problem, turn it over to God. If someone asks, "What are you going to do about it?" just say, "Nothing. I am leaving it to my Lord."

We've all had times when we've said, "I'll do it my way," to God. But His way is always the best way. Ask God to give us humble hearts that we do it His way. When you are in pain, just know there will always be sunshine after the rain. God has a plan and a purpose for everything. Father, please give me the strength to go through this with a good attitude. Help me to keep my joy and peace.

God rules over our circumstances. He may permit a problem to come our way to accomplish a greater purpose we do not see or understand. God worked a miracle of divine intervention on me. He used the skills of the medical professionals to help me. What mattered most is that I believed God was there and was going to take care of me. Through this, I gained a deeper spiritual perspective on my own life that I would not have gotten if I had not gone through this struggle.

> Jesus, cleanse my mind from fear and my body from disease. Touch my body at this time with Your healing power. Give me the wisdom to live a healthy life. Let the power of cancer in my life and in my friend's life be broken. Thank You for all Your healing power. Amen.

You may feel God's promises are not working for you. Every sickness makes us feel as though we are doomed; it's our fault; or that God has forgotten us, that He has others that are more important to look out for than us. Do not refuse to let go of the things that prevent you from going forward. Let go, let God. Just know God never fails, and you are on His top priority. God loves you and cares about you.

We do not have to fight life's toughest battle on our own, and we do not have to face the future alone. God offers rest and joy. It is comforting to know there is someone who is constantly watching over us to protect us from tough battles. God is with you. He can be trusted. He will handle your situation just like He did mine. God is the same whether we are on the mountain or in the valley; therefore, we need to learn to trust and serve Him in good times in order that we might call upon Him in the bad times.

God has a plan for my life, and He will save me. I need to stay in faith and wait for His timing. I need to know God is working in my life even when I don't feel like He is. Sometimes God has a purpose for things that happen in our life. Let God lead, guide, and direct you, and know that God is protecting you.

An example is about two weeks ago. I was in my car, and I fell asleep at the wheel. I went up an embankment into the grass, bouncing up and down, which woke me up. I landed back in the road facing the direction I was coming from. I was so shaken up, but then I thought, *Thank God no one was hurt.* Later, I realized this is going to make me a better driver because I realized that when I start feeling sleepy, I need to stop driving and refresh. It then made me extra aware of other drivers and how important it is to pray for God's protection as I travel.

What I learned from this may be the thing that saves my life someday. This was me seeing from God's view and letting Him show me the truth. This was finding the light in what seems to be a dark situation. It's knowing that because I have God in my life, I can find His light there no matter how dark it seems. God can be in the middle of doing something great for us, and because we are uncomfortable as we'd like to be, we don't even recognize the good things that He has put before us.

Our trials bring us growth. God helps us when we are in trouble. He is always available. When we are suffering, only Christ can replace our resentment with rejoicing. Our whole prospective changes when we catch a glimpse of the purpose of Christ in it all. Take that away and it's nothing more than a bitter, terrible experience. If we will only believe and ask, a full measure of God's grace and peace is available to any of us. We can always call Him, and He answers. We can find purpose in the sadness of our lives. God has a perfect timing, purpose, and plan for our life.

Acts 5:29, says, "Be more concerned with what God thinks about you than what people think about you." God knows best. He created you. Have patience and know that if you take your circumstances to Him. He will give you wisdom, knowledge, and encouragement to get through it. The strength you require will be given to you in your time of need from our Lord. We need to be content and know God is with us. Say this every day: "I am content because God is here with me."

God has had a plan for you since you were born. He is never unprepared. Your present does not worry Him. Your future is not a mystery to Him. You are precious to Him. You are His child.

"Cast all your anxiety on God, because He cares for you" (1 Peter 5:7). He wants you to trust Him even in the face of death. Man may fail you when the going is hard, but God never fails those who put their trust in Him. He is unchangeable. You can depend upon His faithfulness to give you strength to meet each new day with its trials and burdens. So know that suffering is allowed by God sometimes so that we might learn what it means to depend on Him. Also God allows suffering so that we might learn to give thanks in everything. Thank you, God, for giving me strength to get through this day by day, and now I appreciate life more than ever.

"I will be with you; I will never leave you nor forsake you" (Joshua 1:5). "Let go of the Past. Don't think about the tomorrows or fretting about our yesterdays" (Perseus).

Hebrews 13. "I will not in any way fail you or leave you without support." He says, He will not fail you. That means He is in complete control. God is saying that everything will work out because He will not let me down.

Philippians 4:19. God shall supply all your needs. There is a saying, "Today is the tomorrow you worried about yesterday." Let go, let God. If you worry, then you do not trust God completely. We are saying that we do not leave everything in His hands. When we worry, we are saying we doubt God can handle it without our help. God cures all of these three symptoms: mental, physical, and spiritual. If you have the peace of God, you can get rid of your fears and worries.

Seven days without prayer makes one weak. (author unknown)

> Let Go Let God
> My mind was filled with worry and fear.
> My health was starting to fail.
> I had sunk to the lowest point in my life.
> I was a sailboat without a sail.
> I fell to my knees and asked,
> "God, if you're real, let me know."
> A small voice in the back of my head said,
> "I'm waiting for you to let go."
> The moral to this story is simple but true
> I learned after so many mistakes.
> Let Go and Let God do the doing.
> Just remember to always give thanks.
> (unknown author)

Chapter 6

WALKING IN FAITH AND HIS LEADING

Once I took that first step, He then showed me other steps to take. He then taught me how to walk in the light of His truth and love. I then learned to walk away from fear, depression, and disappointment. If I had not walked in His light with this, I would have wandered around in confusion and probably took medicine to help me escape from my emotional pain.

I held God's hand and let Him lead me. He will get me where I need to go to live a long healthy life with my babies. If the path I'm on is crooked, He will make it straight. If I'm headed in the wrong direction, He will turn me around. If I'm at a standstill, He will get me moving. If I'm going in circles, He will correct the course and cause me to arrive at my correct destination.

All I have to do is take step 1—take His hand and let Him lead me. He will get me where I need to go. The road might not be smooth now, and I will fall a number of times, not because God let go of me but because I would have let go of Him. But each time I reach out for His hand, He is always there to help me get back on the right smooth path. I am so dependent upon Him. I trust His leading. This is what a walk in faith is all about.

It is the will of God to heal all who have need of healing. "Lo, I come to do your will, Oh God" (Hebrews 10:7). God has promised us healing, and we have a right to expect Him to keep His promise.

"If you live in me, and my words live in you, ask what you will, and it shall be done to you" (John 15:7).

> Cancer is so limited. It cannot cripple Love; It cannot shatter Hope; It cannot corrode Faith; It cannot destroy Peace; It cannot kill Friendship; It cannot suppress Memories; It cannot silence Courage; It cannot invade the Soul; It cannot steal Eternal Life; It cannot conquer the Spirit. (Author Unknown)

During my cancer, I lost my dad, and now I had to begin to deal with my own mortality as well. I saw things differently.

I need to ask, "What does God want me to do right now in this crisis?" I had to remember God is in control. He is greater than my problem. Some of the feelings I went through, as I said before, were shocking. I was in denial. I felt like I might have caused my cancer. I drained myself with guilt. I had a doctor tell me, "It doesn't matter what caused it now. It's just important to get rid of it and plan to avoid future failure."

Once you believe God is a work in your life, family, or circumstance, you will be able to join Him in the healing process. We may not understand the purpose while we are going through the struggles, but we will eventually see how the circumstance was for our benefit. God gives us grace to face the reality of our problems and grace to help us get through it.

My doctor told me there is a link between having a positive attitude and my immune system. I needed to stay strong and positive, and the Lord helped me do this. He told me that exercise is so important. Getting out and jogging, walking, bicycling, or any moderate form of exertion can help me avoid cancer. Regular exercise is one of the best ways to maintain good health. I read that exercise pumps oxygen to my cells, giving my body added ability to win the war against cancer.

I started praying constantly to the Lord, for I knew He is in control, and I trust His control. He is my inner strength. Without

Him, I could not have made it this far. I prayed and prayed from my heart. Just like I did before with my kidneys and back.

> Oh Lord, please heal me. Cure me of this disease. Touch me from the top of my head to the bottom of my feet with Your healing power. I rebuke the devil ever entering into my body again. In Jesus's name. Amen.

I then made my mind up to try to take care of my immune system more than anything. I want to survive, so I'm going to fight this battle. I realized that focusing on the cause can lead to additional stress. I didn't need to keep stressing and cause another cancer. As I said before my doctor told me it doesn't matter what caused it, it's done. Now just try to get rid of it. I had to stop blaming and judging myself and realize I cannot change the past, and I must concentrate on moving forward.

I needed to calm my fears. I needed to survive this disease. I needed to look at what chemo, surgery, and radiation was going to do for me instead of to me. It is hard, but it can be done with the Lord's help.

> "Say to those with anxious heart, take courage, fear not. Behold, your God will save you." He says, "Call on me and I'll give you what you need." (Isaiah 35:4)

> I say to you, do not be anxious for your life. (Matthew 6:25)

> And Jesus said to him, "If You can?" All things are possible to him who believes. (Mark 9:23)

There is hope through God when we struggle and have battles in our life.

At that time, I started seeing myself as a normal person again. I felt human again. I felt more in control of my body. I was actually doing something good for myself to improve my health. Every day I would push myself to do more minutes walking. As I walked, I prayed. I was challenging myself and seeing positive results. I could see my body improving and feeling my lungs improving. I could breathe better and had less shortness of breath.

The exercise was also a way of releasing stress and tension and gave me a time to pray. It is also an effective way of changing my state of mind. It also stimulates the immune system. Not only was my exercising helping to produce a fighting spirit in me and making me physically stronger, it was stimulating my defense system to go to war more actively against my cancer. It helped me to get well.

When my quality of life improved, my living and beliefs seem to recover. I began to get stronger, and my body was healing. My heart and lungs were getting stronger. I found myself with more energy during the days and sleeping better at night. I have read that since cancer cells cannot survive in an oxygenated environment, and healthy cells thrive on it. The increased level of oxygen being delivered through my blood stream was doing its part in my overall battle against cancer.

> Heavenly Father, please give me courage to face this situation and enough strength in my faith not to go into depression. Help me to sense Your presence in my lonely and dark hours. In Jesus's name. Amen.

I grew stronger with the Lord. I prayed for my faith to grow stronger. Without faith, we can't please God. Faith is the key to which we gain access to Him. We have to have faith to have a relationship within, and believe me, my relationship grew stronger with Him at that period of my life. He was the only one I could turn to for help. No one else could help me like my Lord, not my husband, parents, children, or anyone. I can't imagine not having my Lord to carry me through this. He is the only hope I could see.

God told me over and over again, "Do not be afraid." I trusted God. I traded my self-confidence for God's self-confidence. I held my head high because I knew God's spirit and love was working through me. God was near me, and He heard every prayer. God wants us to cry out in faith when we need Him to comfort us. He wants me to hold tightly to my faith and say, "I can weather any storm."

"The prayer offered in faith will make the sick person well; the Lord will raise them up" (James 5:15). Jesus left the earth with a promise, "I am with you always, even to end of age" (Matthew 28:20). When fear tries to come against me now, I say out loud, "Jesus is with me. I will not be afraid because Jesus said not to. I will remain calm and trust my Lord. I will not fear, for He is with me."

Slowly, as I began turning my burdens to the Lord, my stress began to dissipate as quickly as it had arrived. Stress can have either a positive or a negative impact in our lives. You can become more stress free and feeling like you are carrying the weight of the world on your shoulders if you focus, not on your burdens but on your God. He knows how to use the stress in your life to bless your life. If you don't turn it over to the Lord, you will be desperate to handle this solution yourself. You will not have confidence in God to help you, which means you do not have confidence in anyone to help you. You will feel at times like giving up on yourself, and you have no one to turn to.

I need to take care of myself health-wise. I need to increase my dependence on God daily. The fullest life is found in a relationship, especially when we see He is leading and guiding us. The situation may seem unfair and hard to handle, but know that God knows exactly where you are in life. I will pray for my needs and thank Him for His blessings. I will trust God with every detail of my life. I will read my Bible.

We can read this in Mark 11:22: "Have faith in God." Faith will always move the hand of God. Faith relies on the ability of God. Faith looks directly to the Word of God. Faith knows what God has said because it is in the Bible.

"I will not leave you comfortless. I will come to you" (John 14:18). I have strength and courage even though I never thought of

71

myself that way. My God put this strength in me. As I look back on it, I realize I did what I had to do to survive. I didn't think of it as courage that made me do what I had to do; I thought of it as survival. Now that I look back, I realize that it did take strength and courage to face cancer the way in which I did, courage and strength that I didn't have but which the Lord gave me.

The most important aspects of my life that helped me conquer cancer is my faith in my Lord to get me through this, plus my loving and supportive family. They were all there along with the good Lord, helping me get through all the hard times and treatments, supporting me in every way possible. They were my source of strength and support, my motivation and my inspiration.

Now that my cancer treatments have ended, I have to go back to my oncologist every three months after I receive a CT scan of my chest. It is critical to detect while in an early stage of a recurrence to that area or another area. With all the treatments, I felt like a patient and that the doctors where right behind everything. Now the doctors are going to see me every three months, and having the faith I have is what will get me through this. I have the Lord taking care of me.

God worked a miracle on me. His plan went through as He wanted it to. I now experience a feeling of peace. I feel God with me, and I feel sure that I'm going to be okay. The doctors could never tell me that I'm going to be okay, but the Lord did. He is in control more than the doctors are. The fact is, He controls the doctors with me. I felt His loving care. I know I have rough days ahead, but I also know that my faith is strong. I have an inner sense of peace. I try hard not to be sad or negative. I tell myself when difficulties arise, I have to be confident that problems will last for short period then get better.

I prayed from my heart and on my knees. My confidence grew stronger and stronger that my Lord is taking care of me. The surgeons were able to remove all traces of my cancer, but it was the Great Physician—the Lord Himself—who truly healed me. God made a way for me because I leaned on Him. Physicians may be tremendous help, but in the end, it is our Father God who is always there to provide the help that heals us.

The radiation burns us, the chemotherapy make us feel sick; the special diet tastes horrible. Unfavorable test results sometimes dash our hope. Even our strongest determination is unable to change cancer's oppression. But cancer, doctors, medicine, or special foods don't control my life. God is in control, and His strength enables me to persevere. I need to hold on to Him. He is my shepherd, and He will never leave me or allow me to be defeated. I am in God's hands. He gives me hope.

Doctors like to talk in percentages. If we take this drug with that surgery, then the rate of remission is seventy percent. Sometimes, doctors predict the length of our remaining life as they did mine. They gave me three months. But these are merely educated guesses. Cancer isn't an automatic death sentence. Doctors don't know how many days we will have on earth, but God does.

Fighting a disease like cancer is major. In the course of some chemotherapy treatments, the number of white blood cells in our body can be reduced by ninety-five percent, leaving us with almost no immune system. But God created our bodies with the ability to regenerate white blood cells back to normal levels within days!

Life is a journey to faith. We need to seek God to be a part of our journey. No matter how much preparation you make for your journey, there will be obstacles ahead. Decisions will have to be made, and problems will have to be faced. In all crises of life, there will be lessons to be learned, and through that, you will gain new growth.

The only way to survive my sickness, the death of my daddy in the same year, and my husband's business' failure and see a reversal in what is happening is to surrender them to God. I needed to lift my hands to Him and praise Him.

As my mama said over and over to me, "The same God that helped you find this cancer will get you through it," and He did. He was with me through it all. I am at the top of the mountain. I was healed by the power of God. God works miracles.

Chapter 7

GOD'S MIRACLE THROUGH HIS PERFECT PLAN

Today, I am healed, not by my strength but by God's strength. My life was spared for a purpose, which was God's purpose. In my mind, my life was spared to witness to my family and others. No matter how difficult the journey and how tough the times are, just depend on Him and talk to Him by praying.

Hearing the words, "You have a tumor," was very painful. We can give up, or we can gain new strength of our faith and renew our confidence in God. I wondered if I could go on. I wondered if I could take anymore. My mind was so confused, and I knew my faith had to get stronger. I knew God was in complete control and knew what I needed.

That is how I got through this hardship. He knows the end from the beginning. He will always take care of me. Even though my body was so weak, I needed to remember God knows my circumstances, and He can help me get through anything.

Psalm 50:15. Trust me in your times of trouble, and I will rescue you, and you will give me glory. Life isn't fair, but you can trust God to be fair to you. In these "times of troubles," you can also experience the trustworthiness of God. You'll discover that He's strong enough and loves you enough to rescue you from your circumstances. He will enable you to break free from the anxiety and fear that comes when nothing seems certain.

God has an abundance of blessings for us. Know that when you are scared, we can turn to Him and find His peace. When we are weak, we can find His strength; when we are sad, we can find His joy; when we are in the middle of needing a miracle, He is our healer.

His plan started on the Saturday that I went to the urgent care. It was so evident that He worked miracles on me.

1. He gave me a pain in my arm to acknowledge a problem.
2. I was in a daze and went straight off the exit to the urgent care, not even second-guessing it, which is not like me.
3. He made it where the doctor told me I could go to the emergency room for further testing. If I had gone to the doctor's office on Monday, they would not have had the equipment to find the tumor.
4. It was on a Saturday, so I had to go to emergency room instead of the doctor's office. At emergency room, they gave me a CAT scan where they could not have at the doctor's office. They would have just given me another prescription.
5. He worked through Lisa and Gary, getting me to emergency room to get CAT scan.
6. I was in stage 3A, and the doctor said in a couple more months, it would have been inoperable and spread to my brain. He got me there in time.
7. During the biopsy of my lung, a nurse gave me hope. She was an angel relaying a message.
8. I had no other symptoms. I would have never found this cancer without my Lord. The doctor said I had this cancer already for three years. A couple more months, and I would have been at stage 4 terminal.

Prayer

> Thank You, Lord. I know You did this. Your love took away my fear. Thank You, Lord, that as I take each step, You are always there to guide me through it.

God is my strength! I pray for great miracles of healing. When we honor Him and ask Him for our healing and turn our lives over to Him, that will be the end of worry and fear. Worry robs you of your peace, faith, and joy in life. Jesus said, "If you live in me and my words live in you, you shall ask what you desire, and it shall be done to you" (John 15:7).

We need to be dependent on God's strength. He might be humbling you and testing you to help you in the future. God will not forsake you. There are challenging days full of pain both mental and physical. We all dread that phone call. We pray it doesn't happen. We try not to think about it. It can come at any time, any age. It's like a huge darkness in front of you, ready to take you out. In the blink of an eye, your life changes. Things will change for everyone involved. This can start a new chapter in your life. The future now can't be more uncertain, and no one can answer the question of how, why, and what is to come. All you may be thinking is that things most likely will never be the same.

We hate to think about getting sick, but a health breakdown is one of the inevitable facts of life. We are not promised no sickness. Sin can enter because the enemy hates us. He strikes and causes us suffering and sickness to draw us away from God.

Even if you live a healthy and accident-free life. It doesn't matter how much money, success, or status you have, none of these things can guarantee a healthy or tragedy-free life. Even doing all the right things—such as exercising, eating right, and taking care of yourself—may not stop this day from coming. Even though things are dark and scary, those dark moments don't take away who you were before they occurred unless we let them.

You may be a mess, but you're going to have to think, feel, and behave your way out of it. It is easy to fall into the trap of thinking negative and have self-defeating thoughts that will try to overtake you. Worrying can create chronic stress, which can cause a physical breakdown in your system and eventually lead to a major illness or even death. It is not what happens in your life that makes you feel the way you do, but how you choose to respond. Many of us live on the edge fearing the unknown is what we do. We can't see the road ahead of us; sometimes we envision the worst.

Will I ever regain balance, joy and hope, and vision for any kind of future? You need to avoid talking yourself into thinking the situation is worse than it is. It's not good to have negative thoughts. You already have the answers and wisdom inside you; you just need to learn how to work with it and adapt to the changes so they can take you to a better place than where you started. You need have a positive attitude if you want to change the situation you're in, and the way to do this is growing closer to the Lord and ask Him for a miracle.

The real miracle is that we can be blessed with His healing. Look at your blessings now. Talk to the Lord. You can experience miracles.

Be a survivor. You made it this far; say, "I know I will survive whatever the future holds." Our bodies and minds are programmed to heal. God made us that way.

You will not move forward but will remain stuck. When you play the victim, you waste time, thinking, *Why did this happen to me? What did I do to deserve this?* Your attitude of approach affects everything you do and feel, and it is a filter through which you view the world. It can also influence how other people respond to you and define you. Life can be tough, but we are not victims, at least we don't have to be. We wonder if we will ever regain our balance, joy, and hope for your future. We may live in a dark world, but know that Jesus's light will still shine.

There is no guarantee that you'll be happy for the rest of your life. As you deal with the darkest moments of your life, you will be changed; you will be wiser and more appreciative of the smooth time in your life. Small things don't matter anymore. Why? Because life has been forced into prospective for them. You can find your way back to a life of hopefulness, joy, and love even more. You will live with more passion and purpose. People look back and say that what seemed like the worst event in their life at the time led to some of the best changes that could have happen to them. Life can be tough, but we don't have to be victims. Turn it over to the Lord and trust that He is there for you. Jesus said, "Live for me, and I will take care of the rest."

Things to do:

- Take care of yourself and pray constantly for the Lord to heal you and give you a miracle.
- Forgive yourself.
- Manage your reactions.
- Exercise regularly.
- Practice relation.
- Breathe deeply at least once a day. Repeat a powerful affirmation to yourself several times a day.
- Avoid excessive amount of alcohol, caffeine, fats, and sugar.
- Get high-quality sleep.
- Celebrate a goal you've accomplished at least once a week.
- Laugh at least once a day.
- Take a hot bath.
- Recognize what you can control and what you can't.
- Adjust your expectation.
- Accept what you cannot change.
- Find strength in others.
- Don't get stuck by being negative.
- Let go. Let God.
- Try not to stress.
- Listen to Christian music.
- Take care of yourself.
- Love everyone.
- Have no enemies.
- Do not gossip.

Chapter 8

BOOK OF REVELATION

Back in 2007, I taught the book of Revelation out of the Bible to some of my church members in my home. Just before I taught the class, I went to my preacher and asked for his blessing and permission to do this. I will never forget what my preacher told me. He gave me his blessing and permission, but he also said, "Brenda, you do know that the devil will come after you for your teaching the Word of God to others. The devil might attack you."

My quick response was, "That's okay. The Lord is more powerful. He will take care of me if he does. He is stronger and wiser, and if I am doing the Lord's work, He will bless me."

I taught the lesson for over a year. It went so good, everyone received a blessing through the course. I still hear good reports on it as of today. But Satan did not like this. He does not like Christians. He goes after them. He does not have to go after non-Christians because he already has them in his control and power.

I'm not saying that this is what caused my cancer because I will never know. But it could have been because the doctors said I had cancer approximately three years before I was diagnosed, and I taught the class approximately three years before that. It might have been Satan's work, but God has more power, and He can intervene. He takes control and defeats Satan. God healed me. Thank you, Jesus. I can always trust you!

When the preacher told me that Satan might attack me, I had enough faith to know that God will intervene and take care of me. I had a positive attitude about my Lord then, and I also learned to have one when I was going through the cancer. As my doctor said, it's so important to stay positive for the outcome of my health. My faith only grew stronger from the teaching of the book of Revelation. Being in His Word makes your faith grow stronger. Thank you, Jesus, for my faith in You.

True Christians suffer the most, but know that God will be present in your troubled times. He will get you through this. God says, "My grace is sufficient for thee." If you grow close to the Lord, and you go through a hard time, God will be with you. He comforts strengthens and encourages us. Have faith and let Him reassure you.

The Bible tells us to trust God. He will take what the enemy has meant for evil and turn it into good. Refuse to let the pressures of life steal your joy and peace. The pressures of life can overwhelm us if we let them. So the key is to not let them. Turn to God and His Word. The Lord has promised that He will give us wisdom if we will just ask Him.

Talk with God, and no breath will be lost. Walk with God, and no strength will be lost. Wait for God, and no time will be lost. Trust in God, and you will never be lost.

Believe me, I ask constantly. When I start to thinking, *Why me?* I think then, *Why not me?* I am no better than anyone else for getting cancer. I just have to keep having my faith with positive thoughts.

Chapter 9

My Life Has Changed

Since being diagnosed with cancer, my whole life has changed. I'm living each day as if it were my last. I thought I did before, but I didn't. My every day seems to be so much more valuable. I appreciate life in a different way. A cancer diagnoses reminds us of our mortality. It brings thoughts to our mind of the meaning of life, which many of us do not take the time to think about. You look at things that were huge before as a minute now. You draw closer to the Lord, closer to family and friends. Problems before are not problems now. Complaints before were too little to complain about. Life itself is more beautiful in your eyes.

Strange as it may sound, this can be a positive experience or a blessing. I had to stop and look fear in the face. I remind myself all the time, "Don't give in to fear." Cancer is not the last word. God's Word is! I'm not helpless. I can take positive steps to defeat this. I will look to God in everything I do, everything I say, and everything around me. At this time, I am going to look for His presence in all that I do. He cares for me. He made it happen for me to find it in time. Healing people is Jesus's desire.

I constantly remind myself every day to never forget that cancer is not bigger than God. I can win! The Bible says, "Nothing is impossible with God!" I have a strong faith in God, and I look to Him for a peace of mind and the healing that I need.

The most important choice you'll ever make is whether to serve God or yourself. The good news is that by choosing to serve God, you wind up doing what's best for yourself. When you choose to follow Christ, your faith opens the floodgates of countless good gifts. You receive things like good health, forgiveness, happiness, joy, love, peacefulness, and a future home in heaven.

Through our faith in Jesus, we have nothing to fear. Faith changes how we see the world. From all situations, when you place your faith in God instead of what you see, your heart can't help but overflow with hope. God's power is at work behind the scenes. He's working in both you and your circumstances. He promises to bring something good out of every situation, no matter how bad things may look.

Cancer has changed me in many ways. My outlook on life is so much clearer now. Until my life was in jeopardy, I didn't realize how much I took health and life for granted. Now every day is a gift, and I am so grateful. The future is so uncertain. I realize now that I need to make the most of my time I have. I appreciate my life so much more than I did before I was diagnosed with cancer. I also realize how my strength was from the Lord. He gave me the strength to get through my battles. I realize not to take life for granted now.

Since my cancer, I am going through changes in my life. My eyesight is not as sharp, but now I see God so much clearer. My house is not as active as it was, but I have more time for myself. I am aging mentally and physically, but I am encouraged spiritually, and I know this is just normal. Outward beauty does not last forever. Inward beauty does. Knowing that we may not have another day together has helped us appreciate the one we have today. We don't waste time worrying about the small stuff anymore. We take time to enjoy every sunrise and sunset. God has shown us that life is uncertain so we need to savor every moment of every day. Every day is a gift and that none of us are guaranteed another one on this earth.

My husband works a lot because he enjoys it, but he always takes the time for me. And every minute we are together, I cherish it. The Lord has helped my husband, and I learn as we walked this road together.

I have grown to really love life with a passion. I am grateful for each day. I started reading books, listening to tapes on healing, and eating right. I increased the amounts of grains, fresh vegetables, and supplements. Every morning I lie in the bed, whatever the weather, I am happy to be able to stretch out, pat my dog, and thank God for another day. I love the sun shining, and I love the sound of the rain or the wind moving the trees. When I wake up, I am grateful for whatever time I have. "Hope" is the word that is so important now. With hope, I can do my best to do all I need to do to get well.

"He alone is my rock and my salvation, my fortress where I will never be shaken" (Psalm 62:2). One of the positive aspects of experiencing cancer is that it can be a time to deepen your relationship with Him. You agree, experiencing firsthand, a more complete trust in God: trust for things you haven't had to trust Him with before, trust for things you can't control, what cancer is doing to your body. Believe that God truly loves and accepts you. Ask God to show you what He wants to teach you about Him and about your relationship within. Look to Him for safety and stability during this time of turmoil.

Isaiah 41:10 says, "Fear not for I am with you; be not dismayed, for I am your God. I will strengthen you, yes, I will help you, I will uphold you with my righteous right hand." The opposite of fear in the Bible is not courage but faith. It is our trust in Jesus's presence and coaching that dissolves fear. So when fear ties you up in knots, bring it to Jesus and let Him meet you there. For where He is, fear need not conquer. Fear is Satan's attempt to make you believe that God is small. Fear will always start small, and if you allow it to take root, it will grow. You need to stop fear before it takes over you.

Our challenge is to trust Him and wait for His help. As we do, His presence will calm our fears. Sometimes we feel entangled and react in fear to the Lord. We resist Him, not understanding the help He provides. As you think about your circumstances, are you afraid to turn things over to God? Just know, He is good, and He is near. You can trust Him with your life. The Lord is great. He will keep us calm in the storm.

"Faith comes by hearing the word of God" (Romans 10:17). God keeps us on the right path if you ask Him. Acknowledge Him, and you will see Him moving in your life. Keep your faith and believe. Always trust in God to get us through our problems.

"The unfailing love of the Lord never ends! By His mercies we have been kept from complete destruction. Great is His faithfulness; His mercies begin afresh each day" (Lamentations 3:22–23). "Christ lives in you, and this is your assurance that you will share in His glory" (Colossians 1:27).

Chapter 10

"Fear Not for I Am with You" Bracelet

It was June of 2009. I had just gone through all my treatments (chemotherapy, surgery, and radiation), trusting in the Lord all the way. I started to the pharmacy one morning. The doctors told me there is a chance the cancer will show up in other places, so they want to give me CT scans every three months to start with.

I was so close to the Lord at this time, but as a human, I am still scared. Many of the battles we face today are spiritual battles. I know that when a problem comes our way, we need to replace fear with confidence in God. I do have confidence.

So as I went to the pharmacy, I started praying in the car, "Lord, please help me. I've gone through all this, and I do have faith in You. You helped me find the cancer earlier, and I know You want me on this earth longer. I'm scared now Lord that it might recur again. Lung cancer is said to be high risk to come back. Oh, Lord, please don't let it come back. Please don't let me get cancer again." I cried as I prayed so hard from my heart.

God knew I was scared. I arrived at the CVS and walked in and the people behind the pharmacy counter know me. They said, "Hi, Brenda. I see your hair is coming back." From the chemo, I had lost my hair and some was coming back in.

I said, "Yes, and I'm so glad."

There was a young girl sitting on a chair to the side that came up to me and said, "I heard you just say some hair is coming back. I assume you have cancer. I have a friend that just went through breast cancer, and she has been cancer free for seven years."

I said, "That's great I love hearing about survivors."

She said, "Would you hold your arm out," and I did, and she put this beautiful bracelet on my right arm. "I want you to have this. The Lord is telling me strongly to give it to you."

I said, "I don't want to take your beautiful bracelet."

She said, "The Lord is wanting me to give this to you. I feel the strongest urge right now from the Lord, saying, 'Give it to her.'"

As I looked at the bracelet, I notice it had writing engraved on it, but I could not read it, for I did not have my reading glasses on. After getting my prescription, I asked the girl for her name and telephone number so I can keep her updated with my reports. I thanked her several times and left. When I got in the car, I put on my reading glasses. I cried as I read the words engraved in the bracelet. The words were, "Fear not for I am with you." Chills went all over my body. Thank you, Jesus. You answered my prayer.

I went home and called the girl. Her name was Diane Hogg. She answered the telephone, and I told her she was an angel of the Lord. I told her about me praying all the way to the pharmacy and that through her, God gave me an answer (to not fear because He is with me). She said, "Brenda, this was of the Lord."

First of all, know that Diane did not know what type of cancer I had or when it was diagnosed. She said, "Let me tell you my story. My father was diagnosed with lung cancer in November 2008." That was exactly when I was diagnosed with lung cancer, and that was exactly the month and year I was diagnosed (November 2008).

"He was stage 4, and he died the next month in December 2008." Remember, Diane did not know what type of cancer I had or when I was diagnosed. Her dad was diagnosed the same month and year with the same type. That was amazing to me. Of course, I was in stage 3, where he was stage 4. Thank you, Jesus for helping me find it in stage 3.

She told me she had this friend come up to her during her grieving over her father and said, "The Lord is strongly wanting me to give this bracelet to you." Diane said she wore it for a while and put it on her dresser over to the side.

This particular morning, Diane got up and was getting dressed to go out to run some errands. She said, "I am a real jewelry person. I wear lots of jewelry—a ring, necklace, earrings, etc. But that morning, I did not put anything on except the bracelet. I had not worn the bracelet in months, probably at least a year, but for some reason, I reached over and put it on my arm—no other jewelry.

"I first had to go to my pharmacy close to my home to get my medicine. When I got there, they did not have the medicine, so I went a couple miles down the road, which is close to my house, and saw the CVS, and something told me to go in there and check to see if they had the medicine I needed. They had the medicine, and I was waiting for it when you came in. I had the strongest urge. God was telling me, 'Give the bracelet to her.' It was so clear to me to give it to you."

The Lord heard my prayer on the way to the pharmacy. He had a plan to let me know He is with me. The Lord answers our prayers in different ways. In His plan and His timing. Thank you, Jesus, for the angel you sent to me to answer my prayer and give me a peace of mind. Lord, you are my strength.

I hope one day as I am wearing my bracelet that the Lord gives me that strong urge to give it to someone else. I hope to be God's angel to deliver a message to someone in despair. I try to wear my bracelet every day. It reminds me of God's promise to take care of me.

I now ask God to give me peace and hope and let me know I will be okay. As I pray, I listen to God's answer. He says, "Do not fear, for I am with you." I am convinced that God is with me.

Even now, years later, I have God's words in my mind: "Fear not for I am with you." It gives me an expectation of fulfillment. When God speaks, it's better than any human promise because the very act of Him speaking to me makes it true. The best cure for fear is the word from God. We must choose to believe it. When we put our trust in Him, we can stand on it with absolute assurance.

God sees our circumstances. Take His hand, and He will lead you. Talk to Him and listen to see what He says to you. He will talk to you. Just like He talked to the girl at the pharmacy. I pray I will be quiet and listen for Him to give me the message to hand the bracelet to someone else who needs encouragement.

Before my cancer, I did not stop and listen to what He said to me. I just prayed to Him. I will give you an example of my neglect of not being quiet and listening before my cancer. I went to a doctor three years before my diagnosis, and all I heard was take pain medicine because it's your back aging. No one x-rayed me or ran a CT scan to see the true diagnosis. Who would think I had lung cancer with just having back pain? I did notice that my body was tired and my pain was terrible. I just ignored it and went on taking care of everyone but myself.

Sometimes we need to be quiet and listen to what God is wanting us to do. My mind said several times. *This is not normal. Go and get to the bottom of this problem.* I think back, and that was the Lord talking to me, and I ignored Him. He talks to us through our mind. We need to stop, listen, and do what He says.

It took the Lord's getting me to the emergency room by giving me a terrible pain down my arm. It took my family insisting that I go. He had to work through my family to get me to listen. Just because we can't see ahead doesn't mean He can't. He knew what was ahead and tried to tell me, but I didn't listen to Him.

In Isaiah 41:10, God spoke, "Do not fear, for I am with you; do not anxiously look about you, for I am your God. I will strengthen you, surely I will help you, surely I will uphold you with my righteous right hand."

Though all the physical and emotional pain I've gone through, it has taught me to even have faith more than ever. God is with me. I just quiver when I think today of how God heard me in the car praying and how He answered my prayer.

I kept looking at my bracelet that had "Fear Not for I am with you" engraved in it and felt that peace. He gave me hope. He gave me a miracle. He has done it in His Healing, His Timing, and His Plan. He showed me He heard my prayer of need, and I want to show

Him my gratitude by praying and thanking Him for all my blessings I have received. I try to express my thanks to Him throughout each and every day.

Prayer

> Lord, thank You that I can walk each moment with You, and when I have a crisis in my life, I can put my hands in Yours and depend on You as we walk through it together. Thank You that I feel Your presence in every step.
>
> Lord, help me not to fear. Help me to stop and listen to what You are telling me so You can reveal to me Your truth in my situation. When something goes wrong, help me to listen to You and not jump to negative conclusions. Enable me to recognize the answers to my own prayers. Help me to see the light in every situation.

"Give thanks to the Lord, for He is good" (Psalm 107:1). "The Lord hath done great things for us; whereof we are glad" (Psalm 126:3).

Prayer

> Lord, may I have a greater awareness of Your blessings and express my thanks to You. I praise You for Your special blessings of acknowledging my needs and prayers as You did in this situation. Lord, remind me daily that in Your presence, I need not fear. Thank You that You are my light during this time.
>
> Lord, give me the grace to trust You and rest in Your care. And, Lord, give me the grace to use my words to minister to others. Help my faith in

You be so strong that it naturally shows through me. Amen.

I cried out to Him with my mouth; His praise was on my tongue. If I had cherished sin in my heart, the Lord would not have listened; but God has surely listened and has heard my prayer. Praise be to God, who has not rejected my prayer or withheld His love from me! (Psalm 66:17–20)

God answered my prayer with this bracelet!
Praise be to God, who answered my prayer.

Chapter 11

THE LORD IS MY SHEPHERD

M y son Steve and daughter Lisa were enrolling in a Christian school when they were young. To get into the school the principal asked them a few questions. He asked my son first, "Why do you believe in Jesus?"

I could not imagine what he would come up with as an answer. To my surprise, my son answered, "Because the Lord is my shepherd."

I thought, *What a wonderful answer.* The Lord is our shepherd, and we are His sheep. He leads, guides, and directs us in the right footsteps, which is His footsteps. He loves us, takes care of us, and protects us. I was so proud of my son with his answer.

"What a great answer," the principal said. He was very pleased, and so was I.

How do we experience rest? It comes when we feel secure, as sheep do under a good shepherd, and Jesus offers that security. We don't have to protect ourselves. He's got it all covered. We are simply called to trust Him and follow wherever He leads.

Jesus calls Himself "the good shepherd" who cares for His children. The Bible often refers to the children of God as sheep that are dependent on the shepherd for food and protection. He provides His children with daily needs and protects them, shows them the path of righteousness, and searches for them when they get off course. Then He brings you back to safety of the flock. All He wants of us, His children, is to love Him and believe in Him.

Even if God feels far away, He is always with us, waiting to help those who need Him. We cannot make wise decisions apart from His own wisdom. We do not have the ability to rule our own lives, and we have little success in trying to do so. With the Lord, we can do all things. Have faith and trust in Him, love Him, yield to Him so that no matter what He requires and no matter what happens, you will follow Him. He is our shepherd. Faith is the rock of our stability. If you do this, great blessings will come your way, and whatever you face, He will be with you.

My parents are like my shepherd because they love me and take care of me. My husband is like my shepherd; he loves me and takes care of me. The Lord is my shepherd. He helps me to get through all hard times. My dad's death was so devastating, but with God's help, I am getting through it.

The Lamb (Jesus) who died to save us is the shepherd (Jesus) who lives to guide us. God takes care of His sheep (us the people); sheep follow their shepherd. No better word picture than sheep can be found to illustrate our need for a leader. We are all like sheep (Isaiah 53:6). We tend to go our own way, yet we need the direction of a shepherd. I pray that God always leads, guides, and directs me in His footsteps.

Psalm 23 describes the trustworthiness of our shepherd. He cares for us. He provides for our physical needs. He shows us how to live holy lives. He restores us, comforts us, heals us, and blesses us. He will not abandon us. He leads us through the Holy Spirit, through reading the Bible, and through prayer. He is our leader.

We need to choose to walk with God and prepare for moments of hard times. We may go through hardships, but God promises health to His children. This is the time God wants us to go forward and have patience. Be strong in your faith and know that God is here for you. You are His child, and He is your shepherd.

Lord, You are our shepherd, who leads us and comforts us. You bring blessings to us in the midst of trouble. By getting a close walk with You, You pour out Your strength and heal us. Thank You for all You do. Amen.

For God has said, "I will never fail you. I will never forsake you" (Hebrews 13:5–6). That is why we can say with confidence, "The Lord is my shepherd [helper], so I will not be afraid." No matter how far you've gone into your cancer experience, you already know there are hundreds of questions and concerns to deal with. Who will take care of the kids when I'm in treatment? How will my family get along if I'm too sick to work? What if they find more cancer? When circumstances overwhelm us and we feel like there's no way out, God tells us He is with us. We're not alone. God will always help. No matter what happens or how difficult the moment, you can be confident that God is right there with you.

- A shepherd takes care of his sheep as Jesus does us.
- A shepherd protects his sheep. A shepherd gives his sheep guidance.
- A shepherd looks for the one that is lost.
- A shepherd will die for his sheep.
- A shepherd puts the needs of his sheep first.
- Sheep will not last long without a shepherd. They will wander around on their own, getting lost.

Life would be so much better if a shepherd were looking out for them. It is the same way with us. God wants to lead, guide, and direct us so we can grow stronger in our faith and live the lives He has planned for us. God is our shepherd, so let Him take care of you, protect you, guide you.

"My sheep hear my voice, and I know them, and they follow me" (John 10:27). "All of us like sheep have gone astray" (Isaiah 53:6). Follow His direction, and we will go in the right path.

Chapter 12

HAVE A RELATIONSHIP WITH THE LORD

A relationship with God and religion are different things. Jesus wants a relationship with you. I am not religious. I have a personal relationship with Jesus. Religion is a system, man's idea of God's expectation. Relationship means "the state or fact of being related, connection by blood or marriage."

I am so happy I have a close relationship with my Lord. The closer your relationship you have, the more you will care about the things He cares about, and you will develop a Christ like character. He wants us to become spiritual by becoming like Him in the way we think, feel, and act.

You will never grow a close relationship with God just attending a church once a week or even having a daily quite time. Having a relationship with God means you develop a friendship with Him and serve Him. You share all your life experiences with Him. Include Him in all your activities, conversations, problems, and even thoughts. Talk with Him by praying constantly. Love Him, trust Him, obey Him, have faith, praise Him, and serve Him. Stay aware of His presence. You trust Him and know He is the one in control.

God is faithful, and He will bless those who call on Him. We do not have to fight life's toughest battles on our own, and we do not have to face the future alone. God offers peace to all who will accept it, and He promises joy to those who will take advantage of it. God knows what you're thinking and feeling, so you can be honest with Him. Even if you're feeling angry or betrayed by God, He already knows, and He will affirm His love for you. God wants to do for His people, but first, we must be willing to accept Him by having a relationship with Him and calling on Him. He is going to be faithful to bless those who call on Him.

Cancer may take many things from us, but God can use cancer to heal us in ways we never expected. Cancer may leave many physical scars, but God can heal our deeper fears. Cancer may even take your earthly life, but God will provide a new body and eternal life. Let God's unfailing love begin to heal you.

The importance of having a relationship with God was the theme that also played throughout my parents' life. I thank my mom and dad for all their love and support given to me as a child. They sent me to church and Sunday school, giving me faith in God through Jesus. Faith was important in my family, and it played a major role in my life. My grandparents prayed for my parents, and my parents lived out what they believed and passed it on to my sisters and me. As I said before, faith and prayer are so important with having a relationship with our Lord. Having a relationship with our Lord in return is so important for miracles to happen in our life.

Lord, make us a true reflection of you.

Chapter 13

HAVE FAITH AND YOU WILL HAVE HOPE (YEAR 2010)

Another thing we need is hope. To have hope is having faith. Hope is a wonderful gift from God, a source of strength and courage in the face of life's hard struggles. When we are trapped in a dark tunnel, hope points to the light at the end. When we are overworked and exhausted, hope gives us energy. When we are discouraged, hope lifts our spirits. When we are tempted to quit, hope keeps us going.

As I went through my struggles, I knew I needed to learn to hope and find joy in my life again. I couldn't do anything. This was out of my hands. My family could not do anything. This was out of their hands. My friends could not do anything. This was out of their hands. I wanted words of hope from the doctors so badly. The doctors gave me no hope because they couldn't. They did not know what the future held for me with my cancer, and they could not afford to give me hope. They did not know the outcome.

God is the only one that knows how many days are meant for us to walk on this earth. I knew God was the one and only one that can help me. He knows the future and the outcome. The way I got hope was through the Lord by praying for healing and having a close relationship with Him. He gave me hope.

Setbacks are just part of life. You either fall apart or trust God. When you choose to trust God in handling your setbacks, you will see the good out of it instead of the bad. You will not be fearful or anxious.

Healing starts with your thinking. Nothing will change till you condition your mind to be positive. If you condition your mind to thinking negative, you need to turn your negative thoughts to positive thoughts. It's not easy to go through life thinking of all the reasons why we won't get well. We sometimes think the odds are against us. If you do this, you will get stuck there. God gives us strength for healing. We have to think and know He will help us, but we have to help ourselves for Him to do His work. Put the negative thoughts behind you and reach for a future of spiritual growth.

Part of our life is feeling discouraged and having doubts. Know that when you run into problems and struggles, you will develop endurance and endurance develops strength of character and character strengthens our confident hope. Hope is essential to have during a time of discouragement. Sometimes it takes looking back on the situation before we see how our faith has grown during trials and doubts. Knowing that God wants to use our difficulties to strengthen our faith can help us to trust Him even more.

"Faith comes by hearing the Word of God" (Romans 10:17). God wants us to believe, understand, and explain when we can't see it. If we could see it, it would not be faith. If you have a setback, it's just a setup for a comeback. Lord, give me patience. Let me be strong in my faith and give me hope with the setbacks I face. Amen.

As I think of what I went through with this storm in my life, I realized that my closeness with the Lord even got stronger. I was going through so many questions of worry and anxiety. Why me? What if? What then? What about? Will I? With such a disease, there are questions that are beyond our human ability to answer.

The doctors did not give me encouragement to hang on to. All I wanted was some hope. "Yes, Brenda, you will be fine." "Yes, Brenda, you're going to be okay." I realized that only God knows the future. He is the only one that knows all the results of any action we take. I realized then that the question to ask was, "What does God desire to do in the midst of my situation?" I realized that I must turn this over to God; it was out of my hands.

I prayed to God and said, "I don't know, but you do. I can't, but you can. I'm not able, but you are. Please show me the way." Only God can do this! When something like this comes about in our life that we can't handle, we have to rely completely upon the Lord. He does not want us to worry with bad and negative thoughts. Look for God's direction, and He will not forsake you. He will replace your thoughts with His thoughts.

> May the wisdom of God instruct me
> May the eye of God watch over me
> May the ear of God hear me
> May the word of God talk to me
> May the hand of God defend me
> May the way of God guide me (author unknown)

Hold on to your faith. It takes strength to endure and courage to stand during the battle of life, but the Holy Spirit will give you both. Hope is the gateway of faith—as hope grew, faith grew. As faith grew, fear vanished. The closer I grew to the Lord.

"Do not fear, for I am with you" (Isaiah 41:10). Take away our wealth, and we are hindered. Take away our health, and we are handicapped. Take away our purpose, and we are confused. But take away our hope, and we are plunged into darkness.

There is a big difference between a life of fear and a moment of fear. Know that waiting for God to act can be hard, but when we listen, we hear God's voice through our mind and thoughts. Also through scripture and the Holy Spirit. He will always love us and take away our fear and comfort us. Just put your hope in Him. Follow God faithfully, and He will show you a ray of hope ahead, and your fear will turn into faith and hope. Fear is the absence of faith.

When we put our hope in Jesus, He becomes our reason to believe good things will happen. Pray that hope will remain in your heart for what is to come.

I realize more every day that the best things in life are free. God gives me hope with a positive attitude. Yesterday is a dream of happiness, and tomorrow is a vision of hope. Fear fades as faith grows, and when faith grows, you have hope.

Hebrews 11:1. Faith comes by hearing the Word of God. Many people mistake hope for faith. We hope we get saved, we hope we get well. Know that if you have faith, you will not have to hope. Faith is the substance of things hoped for, and the evidence of things not seen.

"When I had lost all hope, I turned my thoughts once more to the Lord" (Jonah 2:7). I had no hope at first. I had no reassurance. God stood by me. I read in the Bible that God said, "I will never leave thee nor forsake thee. I will be with thee in troubles." I knew this meant that if I suffer, I will not suffer alone. Jesus lives in me. Like I said in one of my testimonies before, when I got my diagnoses, Jesus was with me when He had the angel to tell me everything is going to be okay, which gave me hope, which is reassurance that I needed desperately.

No matter what happens, those who trust in God do hope in His words. Hope reassures us. It is a gift from God. God gives us hope.

"I wait quietly before God, for my hope is in Him" (Psalm 62:5). God will answer your prayers. Always put your hope in his hands. Hope is a wonderful gift from God, a source of strength and courage in the face of life's trials.

When we are trapped in a tunnel of misery, hope points to the light at the end.

When we are overworked and exhausted, hope gives us fresh energy.

When we are discouraged, hope lifts our spirits.

When we are tempted to quit, hope keeps us going.

When we lose our way and confusion blurs the destination, hope dulls the edge of panic.

When we struggle with a crippling disease or a lingering illness, hope helps us persevere beyond the pain.

When we fear the worst, hope brings us reminders that God is still in control.

When we must endure the consequences of bad decisions, hope fuels our recovery.

When we find ourselves unemployed, hope tells us we still have a future."

When we are forced to sit back and wait, hope gives us the patience to trust.

When we feel rejected and abandoned, hope reminds us we are not along…we'll make it.

When we say our final farewell to someone, hope in the life beyond gets us beyond our grief. Put simply when life hours and dreams fade, nothing helps like hope. (Charles Swindoll)

God answers our prayers, and He is the only one that can work a miracle of healing. Your family and friends can pray for you, but He is the one that does it.

- My family gives me lots of love, but God gives me hope from above.
- I can get help from friends I know, but God is with me wherever I go.
- I can get help from family and friends, but God knows what will happen till the end.
- I know I always try to do it my way, but God makes sure I don't stray.

Following God's way is no task; I just need to ask. I ask each day because I know He is with me all the way. God is always there because He cares. Always know God gave us a gift of life, so believe in Him with no sight.

Chapter 14

Fear Fades as Faith Grows

Do not worry because as your faith grows stronger, your fear will grow weaker. You have to have a strong faith to get through these fears. I have faced life feeling guilty, inferior, and rejected at times, which were negative emotions. But now, no more negative emotions, only positive. Emotional bad habits are habits we form. Because we formed them, we can break them.

The first step in breaking our negative habits is to learn the difference between "I can't" and "I choose not to." We need to hold on to God's hand and trust Him to calm our fears. God has a plan for us, and we want to be in the center of it. God knows we can do all things by His grace, so He is trusting in us to trust in Him. If we feel ashamed, He grants forgiveness and comfort. If we feel anxious, He promises to supply all our needs.

We don't know how much time we have on this earth. Only the Lord knows. We need to do our best to make the time we have count. Instead of worrying about what's ahead, let's face it with enthusiasm. Life is short, so enjoy every minute of it. I am so comforted when I know God is in control of my life.

Do you feel afraid and overwhelmed? God is right beside you. Ask Him to help you remember that He's always there with His protection. Tell God what you need and thank Him for all He has done. If you do this, you will experience God's peace.

A doctor cannot prescribe medicine for the peace of God. You need to read the Word of God in the Bible. Medicine can do wonderful things to help a sick person get well, but God knows your body better than anyone. He designed it. Not every prayer for healing may be answered, but know spiritual and emotional healing will take place through God. Just call on Him. Just know that doctors tend to medicate, but our divine healer wants to eradicate.

The enemy of trust is worry. Worrying does no good. It robs us of our peace, joy, and happiness. It does not solve problems; it creates them. When we trust God, worry disappears.

Worry can affect your worship. It can cause fear, hate, guilt, and insecurity. It can make you sick. Worry chokes the Word of God and keeps our lives from being fruitful. God does not want us to worry. Not only is worry a sin and disease, it is unnecessary. We need to give our problem to the Lord.

When we worry, we are doubting God's power. Bring every doubt and worry to God in prayer. Allow Him to transform your doubts into faith and ask God to help you understand the "whys" behind your doubts. He can help you erase each one.

Don't worry. Worry waste energy and time. Be strong and remember your blessings, not your worries. Forget the mistakes of the past and think of the greatness of the future. I heard this person say one time, worrying is like rocking in a rocking chair. You are using energy but getting nowhere. It gives you something to do but gets you nowhere. I know it's hard not to worry, but try to keep your mind busy. You can exercise, clean house, clean closets, listen to Christian music—anything to stay busy and not worry.

There are so many unknowns. How can I handle the nausea from the chemotherapy? How will I take care of household chores when my blood counts are so low, I can hardly move?

Take your worries and convert them into prayer. He will give you peace when you pour out your heart to Him and thank Him for all the blessings He's given. Lord, help me to replace my doubts with belief, my fears with faith, my worries with trust, and my lack of confidence with courage. Help me to focus on You and not my problem.

God protects us. Is there a fear you face? What about the fear of taking chemotherapy treatments and surgery? Radiation? Then, there's the fear of possibly not seeing your children grow up. Take heart; you can face your fears with the strength God gives you. The God who created the universe will help you. He will give you the strength to overcome your fear. Have faith and ask Him for strength.

It has been said that courage isn't the absence of fear but rather facing your fear and going through it. Because of Jesus Christ, you are a child of God. He will never leave you alone. You can face your fears of surgery, of feeling sick, of hair loss, and even the possibility of death with courage. Have faith, and God will always be with you.

Here are a few things you can do to keep busy and not worry:

- Exercise
- Clean and organize house
- Organize closets
- Listen to Christian music
- Read a book
- See a movie
- Paint a picture
- Play a game
- Go for a walk
- Take a hot bubble bath
- Smile and laugh a lot
- Read the bible
- Practice yoga
- Sing songs
- Take a few deep breaths and let it out slowly
- Write a book
- Go to Bible studies
- Volunteer

Look at the cup half full and not half empty. "Don't worry about anything; instead, pray about everything" (Philippians 4:6–7). I heard there are five causes of worry:

1. Fear—there is no cure for fear outside of the Lord. You need to trust Him.
2. Hate—the cure for hate is love, and God is Love. You need to forgive.
3. Guilt—only God can remove the feeling of guilt. Have faith.
4. Inferiority—we need to belong to the family of God. Have a relationship with God.
5. Insecurity—believe in God, and you will feel secure. Have faith.

Hebrews 12:2. Sorrow looks back, worry looks around and faith looks up. Have faith in the Lord, and you will not worry or be sorry for the outcome.

Even though we know the facts about God's love for us and His power to heal, we still experience very real feelings of worry and concern. I heard a saying one time that worry does not empty tomorrow of its sorrow; it empties today of its strength.

Most people focus on tomorrow and not today to enjoy. We always think ahead looking on our to-do list. If we fill our hours with regrets over the failures of yesterday and with worries over the problems of tomorrow, we have not today in which to be thankful.

First Thessalonians 5:17–18. No will of God will ever take you where the grace of God will not protect you! Have a thankful heart. God wants us to not worry. When a farmer sows seeds in his field, it looks like he is throwing the seed away. It seems to be lost, but it isn't really gone. In due time, he gets it back with much more. When we give ourselves to Christ, it may seem to people as if we're throwing our life away. But He said that it is when we lose our lives in Him that we find true life (Matthew 10:39).

Just know that suffering sometimes results from our choices but never because God's love for us has changed. Keep your faith. God shows His faithfulness by always keeping His promise. He has given us His Word and His unconditional love. He continues to keep His promises even when we are no longer capable of keeping ours.

"For the Lord is good and His love endures forever; His faithfulness continues through all generations" (Psalm 100:5).

All of us have our own fears—fear of darkness, failure, unknown, heights, financial disaster, sickness, death. God promises to deliver us from all our fears. We can trust in Him. The only hope we have is daily dependence on the Lord. It's the only way we can make it. Do not worry. Commit this worry to God. When you worry about what you don't have, you won't be able to enjoy what you do have.

Worry assumes responsibilities that you cannot handle. They are responsibilities that God never intended for you to handle because they are His. You have nothing to worry about. He is the one in control, which gives us hope. The Lord is our support. God knows where we are. Sometimes we forget this. Sometimes we even feel that God has forgotten us, but He hasn't. He knows where we are, so when we have these forsaken feelings or feel pity for ourselves of despairing thoughts, go back to the Word of God.

Worry robs you of your joy, peace, and faith. Fear can steal your joy, rob your peace, and paralyze your faith. Depression can steal your joy and peace. It can lead you to worry, fear, and hopelessness. It causes you to see things in a dark area. It makes you feel hopeless. Find your joy in the Lord instead of letting the situation dictate how you feel. Don't let depression control your life. Worry is unproductive; it accomplishes nothing except producing anxiety, stress, and fear.

What to do!

- Start your day with a morning devotion.
- Pray and talk to God and ask Him for His help.
- Meditate.
- Listen to worship Music.
- Exercise.
- Have thoughts on your blessings and not negativism.

Proverbs 23:26 says, "God can heal a broken heart, but He has to have all the pieces." He needs all of you. God wants us to believe when we can't see it. If you could see it, it would not be faith. Things we see are only temporary; what we don't see is forever lasting. Faith is hearing the Word of truth. He is the truth, and the Bible is the truth. Do what God tells you to do and then expect God to do what He said He would do. That is faith! Let your faith grow and your fears will fade.

Prayer

> Dear Lord, I just want to stay in that place of peace. I want to be me again. I don't want to worry or be stressed. I don't want to think, *What if.* Please stay with me and protect me from fear by giving me a stronger faith in You. Amen.

"Fear not for I am with You: Thus says the Lord, 'Do not fear for I have redeemed you, I have called you by name; you are mine'" (Isaiah 43:1). "Be strong and courageous. Do not be afraid or terrified…for the Lord your God goes with you. He will never leave you or forsake you" (Deuteronomy 31:6). "The Lord is my light and my salvation, so why should I be afraid? The Lord protects me from danger, so why should I tremble?" (Psalm 27:1).

> Accept what is, let go of what was, and have faith in what will be. (unknown author)

> There isn't enough room in your mind for both worry and faith. You must decide which one will live there. (unknown author)

> Release the load that God never meant you to carry, and focus on what He has called you to do. (unknown author)

Faith is to believe what you do not see; the reward of this faith is to see what you believe. (Saint Augustine)

Your faith can move mountains and your doubt can create them. (anonymous)

There isn't enough room in your mind for both worry and faith. You must decide which one will live there. (anonymous)

True peace and faith comes from knowing that God is in control. (anonymous)

The hardships and weaknesses that frighten you may be the tools God wants to use to help you overcome this. Allow the Holy Spirit today to turn your obstacles into His opportunities. (anonymous)

Chapter 15

Trust God—He Is in Control

During this time of treatment, my husband's business fell through. He was in the car business. The manufacturer stopped making the cars, so my husband's business stopped selling. But God has everything in His timing and in His plan for him. Doors began to open with other cars. He had doors to open wider than he thought possible. God brought a path of opportunity that was greater than we could imagine. We thought we were at life's end and that we will never accomplish our dreams. We had no idea what God had for us coming our way. Today, he saw God's hand in it. He is happier with the outcome.

Everyone struggles. That is the nature of life. God promises to help us. Everything required for life has been provided through His power and His promises. His Word really can be trusted. He really is enough.

I heard a saying once about a turkey and an eagle.

> That a turkey and an eagle react differently to the threat of a storm. A turkey reacts by running under the barn, hoping the storm will not come near. An eagle, on the other hand, leaves the security of its nest and spreads its wings to ride the air currents of the approaching storm,

knowing that the air currents will carry it higher
than it could soar on its own.

My husband is like the eagle. He spreads his mind to go further.
He never gave up. He could have given in to his feelings and gave
up, but instead, he reached out for answers. He prayed and asked the
Lord to help him. It was natural for him to be a turkey with fearful
emotions, but he chose to be an eagle in his spirit. He spread his
wings of faith, placing his trust in Jesus and Jesus alone, and by this,
his faith for Him has even grown stronger.

I want to live by faith. Looking back over my painful periods
in my life, my conclusion is that God allows storms of suffering to
increase in our life because He wants us to soar higher in our relationships with Him, to keep our focus on His face, to live for His
glory alone, to be more consistent in my walk with Him, to grow
stronger in my faith with Him.

I have spent a lifetime helping people work through their problems. I always felt like a counselor at times. Then, all of a sudden, I
had a devastating problem to deal with. The fact that we are going
through a difficult time may be the greatest indication that God is at
work in our life. We hardly ever learn the great lessons of life when
everything is going well. The real learning happens when everything
goes wrong. That is when God gets our attention.

Many of the struggles we face today are spiritual struggles, and
we cannot win with just our willpower. When trouble comes your
way, you need to replace fear with confidence in God. We need to
replace worry with faith in Him and replace anxiety with His peace.
Trust in God entirely. When the bottom falls out of our life and there
is nowhere else to turn, we will always find ourselves calling on Him
for help.

Human nature drives us to God when we come to the end of
ourselves. Even unbelievers will cry, "God, help me," when faced
with a crisis. I want my children and all children to know that how
we handle our problems is the key to overcoming them. Our reaction will determine whether our problems become opportunities for
personal growth or the means of spiritual and emotional defeat. We

need to handle life's problems with the right heart attitude and know that God is in control of our lives. "Trust in the Lord with all your heart, and lean not on your own understanding; In all your ways acknowledge Him and He shall direct your paths" (Proverbs 3:5).

Chapter 16

PRAYER IS ESSENTIAL

L ord, thank You for me being able to pray to You. Thank You for all Your blessings You have given us. Amen. God is at work in our life. Rarely do we learn the deep lessons of life when everything is going well. The real learning comes when everything goes wrong. That is when God gets our attention. When the bottom falls out of our life and there is nowhere else to turn, we will find ourselves calling on Him for help.

God encourages us to keep praying until He answers. Put your burdens on Him. God has perfect peace, and He will give it to you. When we keep our mind fixed on Him, His power will give us a perfect peace, which is a peace past all understanding. A psychiatrist cannot cure, and a doctor's pills give only temporary relief. But through Jesus Christ, miracles happen every day. Some are ignored or dismissed. Examples are planting of a seed and the birth of a baby. The rain falling at just the perfect time. I could go on and on.

When I was diagnosed with cancer, I was scared at first, but as I began to have strength, I prayed faithfully, and my hope became stronger. As I prayed, I gradually begin to feel God's love and see my glass half full instead of half empty. I prayed that fear and anxiety would leave me. In the midst of my fear and anxiety, God's words in Isaiah 43:4 lifted me up and renewed my spirit. I am close to God, and I know God accepts me as I am. I gained my confidence through this. I can be assured that God will take care of me with my problem.

I ask for strength to face my fears and pain. We can overcome our problems with the strength of the Lord.

Praying is a big part of my daily life. "The righteous cry, and the Lord hearth, and delivers them out of all their trouble. Many are the afflictions of the righteous; but the Lord delivers him out of them all" (Psalm 34:17–19). Prayer is essential. "Keep on asking, and you will be given what you ask for. Keep on looking and you will find. Keep on knocking and the door will be opened. For everyone who ask, receives" (Luke 11:9–10).

God loves to hear us pray. He doesn't require fancy words. There is no minimum word requirement. God wants to hear about our needs and desires. One tiny, simple prayer from us is huge and meaningful to God, who loves to answer our prayers. I know that God answered mine. I could feel it through my inner being.

Even with being the Christian I am and having the strong faith I have in God's healing power, I am as a human still scared. Just the word cancer scares me. I always looked at cancer as a death sentence. Things are better now. Research has come a long way. The best thing I can do for myself is to know that the Lord is in control. My relationship with the Lord is stronger than ever. I constantly pray all day long. I believe we are God's children, and He is going to take care of us. All we have to do is ask Him. In the Bible, "Ask, and we will receive." Also know that there is power in saying, "In the name of the Lord Jesus Christ." If we believe God's Word is the truth, then we may ask for healing in Jesus's name, and we shall receive that for which we ask.

Always believe that God is greater than our problem. Turn all your problems over to Him in prayer. Believe God is there for you. Recognize that depression feeds on self-pity. Acknowledge you have no purpose for staying depressed. Get up and get out and face the world. Exercise and do not stress. Volunteer and get involved with the needs of others. Have a positive attitude, not negative.

You will see yourself praying for others when you don't have to strength to help them in other ways. You will be praying for your country, leadership, churches, your home, your health, and the health of your friends and family. You will be praying constantly for everything and everyone in need. Sometimes, all a person needs is a hand to hold and a heart to understand.

My sisters and I take care of Mom. She is now ninety years old and has Alzheimer's. One day, my sister, Vicki, was sitting on the couch, reading a book, and she heard Mama hollow in the bathroom, "Help, help!" She ran to the bathroom, and Mama was on the floor. She said she was okay but couldn't get up. My sister tried so hard to help her up, but it was impossible.

She ran to the telephone and called her friend and asked him what to do. He said, "Get behind her and put your arms under her arms and bend your knees and try to lift her."

She went back into the bathroom, and Mama was saying, "No, I can't, and you can't."

Vicki said without even knowing what she was saying, "I can do everything through Jesus who gives me strength," and she lifted mama up with her feet dangling in the air so easy. That was of the Lord.

Thank you, Jesus. Mom was okay. She didn't break any bones, just bruised a lot. "I can do everything through Jesus who gives me strength" (Philippians 4:13).

God is always present when I ask for help. When I make a decision, I pray for guidance. The Lord protects me and gives me wisdom to handle the struggle of daily life. Now, I no longer worry about finding someone to lean on. I know I can always rely on God at every moment of my life. He answers my prayers and gives me the understanding and strength to face fears and depend on Him.

Wishing a problem to go away never makes it go away. Action is required on our part. We need to pray hard, stop fighting God, exercise, and take care of our health.

Praying prayers over our fears begins when we release those fears to God and ask Him to help us. God knows your heart. You can always talk to God in your time of loneliness. He will listen. Listen to what He says to you after you pray. You will see He talks to you.

Call on God. "The Lord is close to all who call on Him. Yes, to all who call on Him sincerely" (Psalm 145:18). Airplane pilots can fly in darkness by relying on instruments that tell them where they are and which direction the plane is going. They can't trust their feelings because their feelings are unreliable. We have an instrument to rely on, and it is God's Word. We can't trust our feelings because our feelings change from minute to minute. We may feel that God is far away, but the Bible tells us that He is close to us. He travels on the journey with us. When we feel alone, we can just call on Him. He's right beside us.

Prayers are heard by God. When you pray, believe that you will receive what you are praying for and receive it. God hears us. Prayer is worship. God comforts, instructs, and listens to us. God talks to us by reading the Bible, and then we witness to others. This is what God wants us to do.

As a survivor, I need to realize that one of the biggest mistakes as a believer is to stop praying and worshiping Him. It's natural to do this because we as humans always turn to God more when pain and discomfort gets our attention.

Just know that when you are in a dark valley in your life. Don't worry. Pray and ask God to be with you. He will give you your strength to do what you need to do. You have to stay positive and passionate about what God puts in your heart. Don't let disappointments persuade you to give up. I have learned that every setback means you are one step closer to seeing God work His miracles come true. We need to let go and let God handle it.

We can be on the mountaintop, but life is a journey, and we can go back down in the valley. We need to remember who led us to the mountaintop, and He can lead us back into the valley. If we want to spend more time on the mountain, we need to be careful to be in the Word and pray and worship. It will change your life.

There will be situations coming our way that will try to steal our joy and rob us from our peace and cause our minds to focus on other things. The attack may be just around the corner. Satan never takes a day off. God blesses us and leads us into the future, not us. We have to depend totally on Him. This keeps us close to Him.

Prayer

> Lord, in my difficult times I face, guard my
> heart, guide my words, and show Your grace.
> May I always turn to You in prayer. Amen.

Always know that prayer draws you closer to God. It keeps you in the will of God. Prayer also protects us, gives us hope, changes things, heals us from pain, makes us stronger spiritually, works miracles in our life, and it gives us someone to go to when we are going through trials and tribulations when there is no one else we can turn to for help.

Psalm 84:11. If we are contented we must have everything we desire. God will put in your heart what you need. He puts in your heart what is best for you. "For it is God who is at work in you" (Philippians 2:13).

Matthew 6:10. Your will be done. We want to find out what God wants us to do, not what we want God to do.

"You want something but don't get it. You kill and covet, but you cannot have what you want. You quarrel and fight. You do not have, because you do not ask God" (James 4:2). "Therefore, confess your sins to one another, and pray for one another so that you may be healed. The effective prayer of a righteous man can accomplish much" (James 5:16).

"I have called upon You, for You will answer me, O God; Incline Your ear to me, hear my speech" (Psalm 17:6). "With all prayer and petition pray at all times in the Spirit, and with this in view, be on the alert with all perseverance and petition for all the saints" (Ephesians 6:18). "Rejoice always. Pray without ceasing; In everything give thanks; for this is God's will for you in Christ Jesus" (1 Thessalonians 5:16–18).

Ephesians 5:16–17. Make sure that what you want is what God wants for you, then your joy will be complete.

Isaiah 35:10. The experience of joy has many healing wonders. It strengthens your immune system, burns away impurities, dispenses worries and other negative emotions.

"And the Holy Spirit helps us in our distress. Sometimes we don't even know what we should pray for, nor how we should pray. But the Holy Spirit prays for us that can't be expressed in words" (Romans 15:13).

Ephesians 3:12. Have a close relationship with God through prayer.

> Lord, thank You for every day You have blessed us on this earth. Thank You for our family and friends. Where there is doubt, give us faith. Where there is despair, give us hope. Where there is darkness, give us light. Where there is sadness, give us joy. Where there is hatred, let us love. In Jesus's name. Amen.

Prayer is essential.

Chapter 17

POSITIVE ATTITUDE IS ESSENTIAL

As I was taking my treatments for cancer, my doctors never gave me hope, but they did say over and over, "Your attitude is everything. Be Positive, not negative." If you are positive, you will go forward to better health. If you are negative, your immune system will go down, and your health will go down.

My doctor emphasized on the importance of having a positive attitude, which will give me healthy emotions like love, joy, peace, patience, kindness, goodness, and self-control. He said that certain emotions can lower my immune function. I know that biblical attitudes will help avoid the damaging effects of stress, fear, and worry, which can cause sickness. When the immune system is suppressed, cancer cells can begin to form and grow.

The human response to panic is first we are afraid, second we run, third we fight, and fourth we tell everybody. God's counsel is just the opposite. Don't be afraid; stand still. Watch Him work. Keep quiet. It's then that He does it. He takes over. He handles it the opposite of the way we do it. He waits for us to wait.

I knew that my reaction to this crisis would determine whether my problem would become an opportunity for personal growth mentally and physically and emotionally. I knew I needed "the right heart attitude." Wrong attitudes express our inner frustration with life and our bitterness toward God for allowing problems to come into our life. This is saying that I don't believe God is in control of my life.

Wrong attitudes push us away from God instead of drawing us closer to Him. We need to face reality and take responsibility. We need to know that God's Word will guide us.

The best decision you can make on a day to day basis is your choice of attitude. We need to have a positive attitude. It is more important than our past; our education; our money; our success or failure, fame, or pain; what other people think of us or say about us. The attitude we choose keeps us going or cripples us. When our attitude is right, there is no barrier too high or no valleys too deep.

Try to be positive. Do not be depressed. Try to think of good times and the cup being half full instead of half empty. Praise the Lord for all your blessings you do have. Ask God through prayer to be with you. Most of all listen to what He is telling you and thank Him for all your blessings. Hold on to your hope and wait patiently for God's wisdom, strength, leadership, and knowledge. The only way to live is to die to yourself. Let go, let God.

Friends and family would always look at me and say, "Brenda, you have the best attitude, and you look beautiful. You have a glow about you. You inspire me." What got me through this and gave me the positive attitude was my faith in my good Lord.

"A positive attitude is contagious, but don't wait to catch it from other's. Be a carrier. Be thankful" (author unknown).

Chapter 18

READ THE BIBLE

The Bible is the Word of God, which is our best defense against fear and hopelessness. It is the most powerful book in the world. Listen to the words of the Bible. The Bible says lean on Him, and He will direct you and guide you in the right path. It says to trust in the Lord and lean not on your own understanding; in all ways, acknowledge Him. The Bible is God's guide for your life.

While we experience the blessings of God in our daily lives, life is not without its difficulties, struggles, and challenges. The Bible reminds us that God comforts us in our suffering and troubles. Sometimes, suffering and troubles are His method of shaping our lives and our character. In the Bible, you will find the answers for your journey of life. The Bible speaks to every major problem of life and assures us of God's hope, love, and help. God is greater than our problems, and He can accomplish the best results for our own good.

As I was faced with this crisis, I was scared because I would think of terrible outcomes. When hit with this crisis, I knew I needed to walk with God and trust Him for His healing and deliverance. I wanted immediate healing and to end the dark times by praying and seeking wisdom from His Word and singing praises to Him. I needed His wisdom and peace to give me joy and strength to continue on the path He has set for me. In Proverbs 1:5, it says, "The first step to wisdom is silence and the second is listening"—listen and learn. The best way to do this is by reading the Bible

The Bible is the truth. Believe in the words of the Bible and listen to the truth by reading the Bible. There are actually people that think their way is the only way to do things. Do not be closed-minded. Always be willing to learn something new.

Don't lean on our own understanding. It's not what you do; it's who you are. The Bible is no good unless we put it in our minds and hearts. We are vessels to be used by God. It is not how we look at ourselves; it's how Jesus looks at us. You know what God wants you to do, but unless you do it, you are not obeying God. Don't look at people for what they are. Look for what they can be. Pray for them and witness to them.

Life's toughest problems are not simple. I needed to go to the Bible and read it. It is the greatest resource in the world. These pages in the Bible have endured generation after generation. The Bible offers solid advice based upon the Word of God. It also reminds us that God comforts us in our troubles. It reminds us that God is greater than our problem. As humans, we want to run from our problems. God wants us to use the problem for our own good. In trial or sorrow, God comforts us in all our tribulations (2 Corinthians 1:3–4). With today's problems of the world we need to go to God with them. We do not need to push God away. I need to gain a closer relationship with Him. He is the one and only one to go to for help.

God wants us as Christians to have a confident heart by knowing that He is with you through your faith. God wants us to have a pure heart, and do not do actions out of wrong motives. God wants us to have a forgiving heart. We would be in bad shape if God refused to forgive us. God wants us to have a believing heart. Joy and peace are found in believing God. All we have to do is believe.

Read the Bible daily and pray constantly. By reading the Bible, we accumulate knowledge of God's Word, which is our daily road map and guidebook, which helps us to conquer fear. We need to make the time to talk to God. Tell Him our thoughts and feelings. We need to spend time with Him by reading and studying scriptures. By writing this book, I have spent hours with Him. It has drawn me even closer to Him. I have a stronger faith, which affects my attitude and actions. A daily encounter with God is very important. It is great for our spiritual growth.

We need to align our thinking with God's thinking. We do this by studying His Word and taking it to the heart. God may allow us to struggle—even suffer—to strengthen us. But God does not abandon us. He provides this through people He puts in our paths who encourage us which are people that love the Lord. When we think and act in a humble way, we are then thinking highly of others. The attitude Christ wants us to have always is a Christlike attitude of love and appreciation for those around us, which will enable us to experience a feeling of happiness that only comes from having the mind of Christ.

The Bible:

1. The Bible is a map for our lives, a guidebook that helps you figure out the best route to take.
2. The Bible is a letter from God. It teaches you about Him and His love for you.
3. The Bible helps you to grow closer to Him by becoming more personal and meaningful to you.

Talk to God and stay connected with other Christians and witness to non-Christians. Lord, make me, mold me, and conform me to your image.

Ephesians 3:20. The words in the Bible contains so much life and power. They're stronger than any therapy. God can give you a word that goes back into your past and heal your yesterday, secure your today, and anchor your tomorrow. The Bible is our guide. God's Spirit is our counselor, and His Word is the truth.

Prayer

Lord, help me to become strong in You that
I will not waver or doubt. I pray that I will always

have a teachable heart that recognizes Your hand
in my life. Help me to trust Your timing. Amen.

"He gives power to those who are tired and worn out; He offers
strength to the weak. Those who wait on the Lord will find new
strength. They will fly high on the wing like eagles. They will run
and not grow weary. They will walk and not faint" (Isaiah 40:29, 31)

The Bible is the truth!

Chapter 19

SHOW LOVE AND SUPPORT TO ONE ANOTHER

My parents loved the Lord and raised us to love, trust, and serve God. Through good times and bad, they simply trusted God. They worked hard and provided a safe place for us spirally, emotionally, and physically. Parents can provide a safe haven for our families with the help of our Lord, whose love for His children is strong.

> Blessed is the man who fears the Lord, who delights greatly in His commandments. His descendants will be mighty on earth; the generation of the upright will be blessed. Wealth and riches will be in his house, and his righteousness endures forever. (Psalm 112:1–3)

God shows us love every day and wants us to show our love. This is something all of us should do. Let our loved one know how much we respect and love them. There is not a day that goes by that I do not tell my parents and children that I love them. I try to tell them every day and show them in every way.

My daddy was well loved. My niece, Morgan, wrote this as an essay at school and wrote this before he passed. I am so happy that she expressed her love to him. She named her essay, "The Twinkle in His Eye."

* * * * *

The Twinkle in His Eye
Morgan Maris
(10/20/1999)

"I love you, baby," he says as he holds my hand in his with a warm, welcoming smile on his old and beautifully aged face.

"I love you too, Papa," I respond. During my entire life my grandfather has always reminded me that I am loved and I, likewise, love him. I have always shared a special bond with my grandfather and, through my eyes, he is a "genuine hero."

His name is simple, George W. Carlisle, and he is very special part of the lives of my family. When I say family, I don't necessarily mean just my immediate family but the entire tree, the whole clan! Whenever I think about my Papa there is always pleasant, prideful thoughts that fill my heart, for he is one of my favorite people to be with in the world!

Just the other day I was thinking of how fortunate I was to still have a special grandfather in my life such as my Papa. There are many young people about my age that don't have relationships with their grandparents for different reasons.

There is an enormous respect that I have for my Papa, not just because he is an elder but because of the many roles and duties in which he has played throughout his life. Not only has he succeeded in raising three daughters, one of them being my mother, but he has fought for our country in WWII which, in the end, left him in a struggle to overcome the many harsh and cruel experiences which he had a part. He is fortunate and proud of what he has accomplished throughout his life. I have never once heard him complain or wish life away as I hear so much these days from people around me. I am proud of this man that is my grandfather who has always had a simple and positive attitude towards life. He lives life day by day, never worrying about the little things that stress out my Granny! My grandfather and I look at life in the same light that everything happens for a reason.

Whenever he walks into a room, he brings along with him this smile that is enough to brighten anyone's day! There is a special twinkle in his eye that makes him look as if he were an "angel" never failing to brighten mine! At Christmas time Papa will walk through the door saying, "Ho ho ho, Merry Christmas!" and the family is always delighted to see him arrive, adding that little spark to the moment. There are just not enough words to describe how special my Papa is to me. He may not be the richest man in the world or even the most intelligent to anyone, but to me, he is the best grandfather that anyone could ask for and he is mine.

When I grow older I hope to be just like my Papa with the same amount of energy and liveliness that he possesses. I want to still be able to climb in and out the car, going to yard sales on Saturday mornings, and laughing and singing with such excitement that nobody will be able to guess how old I am!"

It is said the "old age should not be measured by the years but how much energy one has!" And of course, I would never forget the last, but most important thing I'd wish to have, which would be that special "twinkle in my eye!"

* * * * *

My daddy was so happy when this was read to him. It meant so much to him to know he was loved that much. We should always show our love and give our time to our loved ones as Morgan did. This is being Christlike. God is love.

"A new command I give you: Love one another. As I have loved you, so you must love one another" (John 13:34).

Picture of Daddy (twinkle in his eye)
George Wesley Carlisle (1917–2009)

Chapter 20

THREE YEARS OF SURVIVAL (YEAR 2011)

I do believe as you age or have a crisis, you can become more mellow and Christlike. The trouble is some people wait till they are at a very old age before they begin to really have a peaceful, happy life. Now at my age, my eyesight is not as sharp as it used to be, but I have never seen God's love more clearly, and I have a stronger relationship with God. At one time, I thought I was indispensable, but now I realize more than ever that I am not. Without Him, I can do nothing. He is my strength.

I see people in a humbler way. I see babies, old people, and animals as at our mercy. I'm quicker to help them. I see a dog lost and will go a mile out of the way to find the owner. In the last few months, I have rescued three dogs and found their owners. My love flows out for the needed. I love people and animals. I am much more aware of other's hurts and pains. I take more time now to enjoy life. I am finding that walking and praying help me physically and spiritually. I work harder than ever trying to take care of my health. I think more of myself and my heath than I ever did. I try to eat right and exercise. Water aerobics is good for me. It gets my heart rate up and doesn't tire me so fast. I have learned that things do not define who a person is nor do they imply a personal worth.

I no longer have to accumulate a lot of clothes, jewelry, or money to be happy. Knowing that my life is a vapor (can end fast) encourages me to become goal-oriented and to fulfill my God-given purpose on this earth.

Mama always told me that everything happens for a reason and that the same God who helped me find this cancer in stage 3 instead of stage 4 will be with me till the end. She also said there is an assigned time for everyone to pass, and I will not go till that time. She said the Lord wants me to help others get through this and to look at me and think, *By Brenda's having strong faith and God's answering her prayers, then He can do the same for me.* And He will. Just ask Him. Have a relationship with Him. You are His child, and He loves you.

I hope and pray I never have to go through cancer again. I am stronger and better now. I have a lot more confidence and faith in myself. I am a stronger Christian. I know I can do anything with God's help. He is my strength. Without Him, I can't imagine what my life would be like.

When you receive God in your life, it's not a task to live for the Lord. He lives through you. You will be a changed person. You will always have God beside you in your good and bad times. Ask Him to show you what He wants to teach you and how. He wants to change others through you.

People look at me and say, "Brenda, you amaze me how you came through your diagnoses, treatments, and struggles with cancer." They say I am an inspiration. I tell them it's because I had the Lord with me. He comforted me, supported me, loved me. He listened to my needs, and He cured me. I trust God to be with me through upcoming difficult days.

Self-pity and despair can overcome even the strongest of us in times of trouble. I focus on Him and pray. He hears my prayers, and I rise above my situations. I listen to Christian music. It can change your life. While listening, your thoughts are not on thoughts dwelling on failure, disappointments, and discouragement. Your mind and heart focus on the Lord and His Glory and even makes your relationship with Him closer. The Holy Spirit can bring songs of praise to my mind at the moment I need it most. Rather than needing medication, I need Jesus. Lifting my praise to God helps me to release my love for Him and forget my problems. I joined the YMCA and exercised. This helps me mentally and physically, also spiritually because praying is better than worrying.

Prayer

> *Lord, so many times it seems as if a thief is*
> *trying to steal my peace. Life can be overwhelming*
> *at times. The news is so discouraging. There are so*
> *many problems in the world. I ask that You keep*
> *me in perfect peace. Let my mind be steady and not*
> *racing. I need Your strength in me. Amen.*

"Peace I leave with you; My peace I give to you; not as the world gives do I give to you. Do not let your heart be troubled, nor let it be fearful" (John 14:27).

"God comforts us in all our affliction so that we will be able to comfort those who are in any affliction with the comfort with which we ourselves are comforted by God" (2 Corinthians 1:4).

"You will keep in perfect peace all who trust in you, whose thoughts are fixed on you!" (Isaiah 26:3).

"I will hear what God the Lord will say; For He will speak peace to His people, to His godly ones; But let them not turn back to folly." (Psalm 85:8).

"Therefore, having been justified by faith, we have peace with God through our Lord Jesus Christ" (Romans 5:1).

"If possible, so far as it depends on you, be at peace with all men" (Romans 12:18).

"And the peace of God, which surpasses all comprehension, will guard your hearts and your minds in Christ Jesus" (Philippians 4:7).

"No eye has seen, no ear has heard, and no mind has imagined what God has prepared for those who love Him" (1 Corinthians 2:9).

"For I know the plans that I have for you, declares the Lord, plans for welfare and not for calamity to give you a future and a hope" (Jeremiah 29:11).

Romans 12:12. Be glad for all God is planning for you. Be patient in trouble, and always be prayerful. Cancer is a disease in which cells grow faster than they should. Chemotherapy works to eradicate all the cancer in your body by killing only fast-growing cells. Since your hair is a fast growing cell, it falls out. While it may be frightening to see your hair falling out, it's part of the plan to help you. It means the cancer cells are being destroyed too. Certainly cancer wasn't in your plans, but God has plans to help you. He knows your hair is falling out, but He uses things like chemotherapy to kill the cancer in your body.

Pictures of me and Abby (2009). Abby was always taking care of me!

Chapter 21

ENJOYING LIFE

*A*s the day ends and I lay my head down on my pillow, I will thank God for the best day of my life. Once you have fought something like cancer and won, there's not much that's scary. I looked death in the face. Fear now plays less of a role in my life than it did. Trials and tribulations can really make you stronger. Health is a choice. We choose to be healthy and have joy and happiness. These are all chooses that we make when we have the power to choose. But in order to feel that power, we need to learn to lean on our Lord for strength and love the Lord with all your heart, which makes us love ourselves. When you go through cancer, and you are a survivor, you love yourself and life so much more.

Joel Osteen once said, "Don't just go through it, grow through it." It's so true. I have grown mentally through all my struggles. I have learned that life is short. We need to live each day the best we can and be happy one day at a time. We need to live the life God intends us to live. After coming so close to death with this cancer, I look at things so different in life. I want to renew my strength by thinking positive through my thoughts and words.

For the rest of my life, I want a life filled with peace, joy, and happiness. I want to read scriptures and pray to Him. I want to live my life each day to the fullest. I want to listen to what God is saying to me through Scripture. I want to improve my thoughts, actions, and attitude with God's help and guidance. He can help me have a life that is meant

132

for me. Since my survival of this cancer, I have learned to enjoy life. All it takes to begin to enjoy life to the fullest is your decision.

God has shown me that the life He has given me is meant to be enjoyed. We need to enjoy our journey through life. He wants us to not fear, stress, worry, have anxiety or depression. God is not impatient. He wants us to enjoy our home, our friends, and our family. All it takes to enjoy life to the fullest is your decision. Below are decisions you need to make.

Know that life is Good. Put off feelings of inferiority, and people will see you different. God created you the way He wants you. You might not be better than anyone else, but you are just as good as anyone else. Have strength and power to love yourself. Carry yourself with pride. Have confidence in yourself. You don't have to have the most talent, be the prettiest, or the youngest. All you have to do is be kind, friendly, and confident, and you will stand out. You may say, "I struggle with temper, etc." God approves you. People see you the way you see yourself. If you start loving yourself, other's will love you. If you see yourself pretty, other's will see you pretty.

> You are who you are for a reason.
> You are part of a plan.
> You are a perfect design.
> You look like you look for a reason.
> Our God made no mistakes.
> He knit you together within the womb.
> You are just what He wanted to make.
> The parent's you had are the ones He chose.
> And no matter how you may feel,
> They were custom-designed with God's plan in mind.
> And they bear the Master's seal.
> No, that trauma you faced was not easy.
> And God wept that it hurt you so;
> But it was allowed to show your heart,
> So that into His likeness you would grow.
> You, are who you are for a reason.

You've been formed by the master's rod.
You are who you are, beloved,"
Because there is a God! (author unknown)

Don't feel guilty because it will make you do worse. Shake it off. The most important opinion you have is the opinion you have of yourself. You are growing. Don't listen to people bullying you. If you do, then you are listening to the devil. If you listen to him, then you are not doing what God intended you to do. God created you the way He wants you. You brag on others, but make sure you brag on yourself. You are smart, talented, and beautiful. There is something special about you.

Don't be negative; be positive. God loves you! Look at the cup half full instead of half empty. Your gifts, talents, and right people will come around you if you start loving and thinking of yourself as the highest. After my diagnoses, I found myself with all kinds of questions and thinking negative. Don't be defeated. Clear out negative thoughts. You need to think positive to fight cancer. Your mind controls everything. Don't dwell on every negative thought in your mind because that is the enemy trying to control your mind. Don't let your thinking limit you. Think positive because Jesus is positive and not negative. I'm healthy and happy. Everyday, say this to yourself, I'm strong and can handle anything that comes my way, through my Lord.

Take care of yourself and be happy. Take what God has given you and make the most of it. Be happy with who God made you to be. God loves you who you are. Pray and ask God for strength. He will guide you. We always need to start our day out in faith, thinking positive thoughts. Happiness is not looking for what you want but being content and happy with what you have. Happiness is a decision you make, not an emotion you feel. There will be struggles in our life, but we must make a decision to be happy. Heavenly Father, give me a positive attitude. Give me a greater vision of your love and guide me as I walk through dark valleys and remind me that I need to fear no evil. Thank You for Your love for me and my love for You. Amen.

Fear Not. We can't get thoughts of fear like, *Why is this happening to me?* Say, "My God is with me." Get up in the morning and say, "Lord, thank You for another day." My mom is eighty-seven years old now, and every time she mentions her age, she says right after it, "I am so blessed. The Lord has been good to me and blessed me for being here on this earth so long." If she feared her age, she would have started looking at it with anxiety. She sees it as a positive blessing instead of a negative fear. She is so close to the Lord that she does not fear death. She says she will be in heaven, so she does not fear it.

Witness. Sometimes, telling others about Jesus can be difficult, especially in today's world. We often fear rejection, mockery, and even persecution. But if we resolve to let Christ live through us, we can be enriched and enrich nonbelievers. We can make a difference in this world. This way we can show light into dark situations. People are watching us whether we realize it or not. They want to know if being a Christian really works when we face lives toughest problems. Our pain and problems sometimes are the messages by which God gets their attention as well as ours, and our faith is the response that He uses to speak deeply and powerfully to our hearts. As people watch how we deal with life's problems, they begin to realize the power of prayer. We can witness this way.

Be grateful. I am so grateful. I am choosing to focus on possibilities, which means I am looking forward to the future. I have a good attitude and outlook on my future. Because of my Lord, my faith in Him is so strong, and "I fear not because He is with me." Lord, thank You for all my blessings.

If you make a decision in your life to follow these steps, you will enjoy life and be happy.

Picture (2009): fortieth wedding anniversary

Picture (2019): fiftieth wedding anniversary

Chapter 22

So Blessed
(Year 2013)

I t's been five years this year. Today is March 2013. I'm still here because of my Lord. I appreciate every day more than ever. I see every day as a gift from God. I don't take anything for granted. I think about how my life could have been gone in a moment. I am so grateful for the opportunity to experience each day. I don't want to complain or focus on what's wrong. I want to live each day to the fullest. There is no guarantee that we will be here tomorrow. I know now things may not be perfect, but life can be a whole lot worse. I now live every day as if it could be my last. Thank You, Lord, for my life. I appreciate it more than ever.

My doctor told me I am cured. Thank you, Jesus. My husband and I are so happy to hear these words. Five years ago, I was scared, but the Lord comforted me through it all the way. He revealed Himself to me through our prayers. He watched over me every moment of the way. He sent His angels to rescue me and comfort me. He blessed me with His presents and words: "Fear not for I am with you." Not only with scriptures but with the bracelet that the girl gave me at the pharmacy. He had compassion on me and what I was going through. He helped me gain wisdom through His Word. My life is prolonged by Him with His healing and His plan. He helped me gain confidence by having faith and trust in Him. I am healed because of Him and Him only.

God is allowing me to enjoy the blessings of life. He spoke to me and said, "Brenda, you are a witness. Write a book." So here I am. Today, I am healthy and strong. I saw the hand of God in my life. He brought me out of a difficult time. He protected me. He turned a negative situation into a blessing. He always supports us with never failing love. Even when things don't go as we desire, we know God loves us still, supports us through the best and the worst of times. We are all God's children. I am thankful we serve a God that can handle our problem no matter how big or small they are.

How we respond to our challenges tells people what we really believe. As I gradually regained my health, I realize that God was working in my life, but even more in the lives of others. Those who prayed for me, sat with me, called me, comforted me, they all began to share with me what God was doing in their lives as they watched our faith being put to the test. We learned that God was at work in all this.

We should be excited to tell our family and friends and even strangers about God's promises and love. When we pray about sharing the good news, God will give us the wisdom and opportunities to do so. He will bless you because He knows you are faithful, and He will let those blessings flow from you to others. This is your way of witnessing. Being faithful makes others faithful. God blesses you so that you can bless others.

Prayer

> Lord, give me ears and a heart to receive Your words. It's through You we have life and peace and healing. Lord, my greatest happiness in life is knowing who You are and our relationship. Lord, thank You for the peace that is in me mentally, emotionally, and physically. I can breathe easier now. I can relax, and I can smile again because I know everything's going to be all right. You are in control. Amen.

One year ago, my husband, and I sold our house and moved in with my mom. She has Alzheimer's, and we are taking care of her. We are at this time building a house on the lake and enjoying every minute of it. In a few months, we will be moving into our new house, and I can't wait. We want my mom to move in with us. She is eighty-seven as of today. Today is her birthday (October 20, 2013). She is an angel. My husband loves her as much as I do. She loves him. She said he is like a son to her and not a son-in-law. I thank God for this time to enjoy my mom. We are helping her, and she is helping us by living with her.

My children and grandchildren are all healthy and doing good. I thank God for them. I have three grandsons and one granddaughter. They are looking forward to the new house also. God is so good. He has given me more time to be with my loved ones. Thank You, God. Thank You with all my heart. You are helping me to fulfill my dreams.

I set new goals and realize life is so short. Money and material things mean nothing to me now as much as fulfilling my God-given purpose on this earth. I'm enjoying my grandchildren. My faith has grown. During my life over the years, I have become wiser, more sensitive, compassionate, generous, and humble. I want to celebrate the gift of life every day, and I'm just so happy to be alive.

Some people believe that the best things in life are expensive. Just know that the best things in life are not things. The value of family, friends, and faith points us to the realization that what matters most in life is all wrapped up in people and the Lord. We do not hold them in our hands but in our hearts. Our greatest riches are the riches we have in Christ. Having a personal relationship with Jesus lights up our life. The more you walk in the light of the Lord, the brighter it gets until it lights up every part of your being. In the light of God's love, we can find strength, help, and courage. Then when He takes our hand, He can lead us anywhere. The unknown is frightening, but when we have a relationship with the Lord, we can know He is in it. His love takes away our fear.

He gives me joy when I'm discouraged. He opens a door when I can't see out. God is fair even though life is unfair. I have a new sense of prospective after fighting for my life. Now I chose to be happy more than ever. I have been through so much. The cancer plus the death of my dad. My strength, I will truly say, is "my Lord." My goal during the battle of cancer in 2009 was to have enough strength to just take a shower. I had no strength in my body. I would look in the mirror, and I looked like death. I was as pale as a white sheet, I looked old and tired, but with the encouragement of my family and the strength of my faith in my good Lord and His miracles, I regained my health.

Sometimes when were in the middle of the questions, worries, and needs of our lives, we may lose sight of the obvious. We all experience storms, and Jesus doesn't always prevent them, but He has promised never to leave us nor forsake us (Hebrews 3:5). Also, in Proverbs 24:16, it says, "Falling down doesn't make you a failure but staying down does."

There was a saying one time I saw where a donkey fell down in a well. This man came along and started throwing sand in the well to fill it up, not knowing the donkey was in there. The donkey stood over to the side, and each time the man threw a shovel of sand on the donkey, the donkey would shake off and step up on the pile. The donkey kept shaking off and stepping up till he stepped out of the well. He could have just stood there and been buried. So just shake off and step up, and you will be fine. Also, in Luke 9:62, it says, "Life is understood by looking backward, but it must be lived by looking forward." Always go forward in life. Don't stand still.

The Lord gave me hope, not the doctors. The Lord kept my attitude strong. I share my feelings more openly. I take vitamins, eat better, and exercise more often. I pray constantly and my love is more open. I take more time for myself, worry less about pleasing others, and know more clearly than ever that each day is a treasured gift to be lived to the fullest.

I don't want cancer on anyone. It is a nightmare, scarier than anything I could ever experience. I pray I never get it again, but the physical and emotional pain taught me to really love life with a passion. I have learned, after having cancer, not to take things too seriously. Life is temporary. I need to take advantage of every minute of it. I always look at more things positive. I notice the beauty of life more, like the grass and trees turning green, the beauty of the flowers, the sky, stars, moon, the clouds. I praise God for these treasures. Simple pleasures bring me great happiness. I have an inner peace within. I try hard not to be sad or stressed. When difficulties arise I feel they will not last long.

My caner diagnoses gave me a new life of seeing the world. The Lord took care of me, and He always will. I am enjoying my children and grandchildren so much now. I love being with my family. We are closer than ever.

It has been five years now since I was diagnosed with cancer. I went to my oncologist, and he just released me. He said I can go every year if I desire just to visit him. I don't even have to get CT scans again. Part of me still wants to keep going to him since I have felt secure with them and My Lord.

My oncologist said, "Brenda, when all the doctors met for your case five years ago, there were five of us. All wanted to do different formulas of chemo, but they went along with the one I suggested. There were two chemicals for the chemo I came up with. As you see, it worked." This was the Lord. He put me in good hands.

"Behold, I am with you always" (Matthew 20). "Before you call, I will answer and while you are still speaking, I will hear" (Isaiah 65:24). Thank you, Jesus, for helping me find my cancer in time, putting me with the right doctors, and conquering this terrible disease. This was Your work again taking care of me. You did it, and I praise You for it. Amen.

It's amazing the times I can see God's hands working with me. I needed Him. No one else could do anything for me. It had to be Him. I do not know what people do when something happens to nonbelievers to get through situations like this. It would be a terrible situation.

Oh, Lord, thank You for being my Father and getting me through this. Amen.

Chapter 23

QUESTIONS THAT I CAN NOW ANSWER (YEAR 2014)

In this book earlier, when I was first diagnosed with cancer (2008), I wrote questions that came into my mind. Now, six years later in 2014, here are the answers to those questions.

What job can I do now? Will I be able to work again? Will I be able to cope with this emotionally and physically? Should I set goals? Yes, I can do anything. There are no changes in my knowledge or work ethics from before the cancer till now. I can hold down any job that comes before me. I am strong and energetic. I am willing to take on any challenge. My emotions are strengthened physically and mentally. I know more than ever that my Lord took care of me then, and He is taking care of me now.

Will I always be a cancer victim? What do people think of me now? Will people always look at me as a cancer survivor instead of Brenda? Will I have a normal life again? Will I ever feel like Brenda again? No, I will not always be a cancer victim, and no, I am not looked at as a cancer survivor. Yes, I feel like Brenda again. I look the same as before, feel the same if not better. I am very happy. No one knows I have had cancer unless I have told them, and the ones I have told love me even more and never look at me that way. They treat me the same and are thankful they have me here to enjoy life with them.

Should I clean out my closets so my children won't have to do it? I remember thinking I might die at the beginning of this cancer and this came in my mind. Yes, I did start cleaning out my closets but only because I wanted to stay busy and not think of the disease. It is the best to stay busy and keep your mind off it as much as possible. Just pray and talk to the Lord, listen to music, and try to keep a peaceful mind though it.

Will my hair come back? Yes, it came back right after my chemo was over. Very thick and pretty.

How long do I have to live? How long will I be with my grandchildren and children? No one knows how long we have to live. Even now, I don't know. People that have never had cancer do not know. Just know, if you are having scans and believe in the Lord, then you are better off than even the ones that don't know whether they have cancer or not. You are doing what you have to, to take care of your life.

Will my parents at their age be able to cope with this? Am I putting too much pain on my children, husband, and family to go through this? My family is fine. As I said before my dad died during my cancer treatments. He was not well before he found out I had cancer. He was very weak and tired. He was reassured from my sisters before he died that I had a successful surgery, and I was doing fine. I went to see my daddy in the hospital just before my surgery and prayed a Savior prayer to him. My family was all around his bed. We all prayed together, and he had a sweet smile on his face.

I miss my daddy, but I know he is in heaven now with our good Lord. When my father died, it was so devastating. My mom looked so frail. I wondered how she would get through it. She surprised my sisters and me by walking around like in a daze, not even crying. I know this was the Lord with her. He was putting her in this state of being to help keep her calm. He was right beside her all the time. My mom is fine, she is still with us now and an angel on earth. My husband and children are still here supporting me.

Our grandchildren George Michael, Alexis, Dalton, and Tucker are so precious. I thank God every day for giving me time to enjoy them. I pray I have many more years to enjoy them.

Top left: my children Lisa, Steve, and myself.
Top right: my mother and mother-in-law, Alice Carlisle and
Berlene Brandon. Bottom, left to right: me, my sister Vicki,
Mama and Daddy, my sister Judy, and my sister Jeanette.

Chapter 24

TRANSFORMATION (YEAR 2015)

L et God transform you into a new person by changing the way you think. You may be going through divorce, death, sickness, trauma, financial problems, rejection by others, lack of support from coworkers, betrayal of a friend, unsaved loved ones, uncertainty of future, fear of failure. Whatever you go through, know that change starts first in your mind. The way you think determines the way you feel, and the way you feel influences the way you act.

When I first got cancer, I was saying, "Why me," but why not me? I had to look at reprogramming and renewing my mind in a different way to be healed. I had to transform my mind to knowing God is going to take care of me if I turn it over to Him. To do this, you need to stay focused on positive things in life.

The choice is up to you if you want to think positive or negative. You don't have to dwell on every thought that comes to your mind. Think, *Is this thought coming from God or the devil? How can I tell?* If a negative thought, it's from the devil. If it brings fear, worry, doubt or unbelief, and makes you weak or insecure, get rid of it. Don't dwell on it. Choose to think of something positive. God will help you to think the right thoughts and actions during a transition.

Right actions can change your character, and God will lead you to be a better, calmer, and happier person. You will then enjoy your life because God will be with you to guide you in the right path. Ask God for wisdom, peace, and guidance.

My doctor emphasized the importance of having a positive attitude, which will give me healthy emotions like love, joy, peace, patience, kindness, goodness, and self-control. These are important to keep me calm and less stressful. He said that certain emotions can lower my immune function. I know that biblical attitudes will help avoid the damaging effects of stress, fear, and worry, which can cause sickness. When the immune system is suppressed, cancer cells can begin to form and grow. Also, you are not letting God work on your healing if you stress and worry.

Being transformed is the beginning of living an extraordinary life with a closer relationship with God, a life of peace, hope, calmness, joy, fulfillment. You will love Him with all your heart, and your love will grow stronger. You will catch yourself praying more and communicating with God more. Every time you pray and praise God, your relationship gets closer. God becomes your communicator, your best friend, your Father, your protector, your supporter, your everything. God will keep growing us and changing us. God is faithful, and in His timing and in His way, He'll do it.

When you start living in Christ, you look at life with new understanding. When Christ fills you with the Holy Spirit, you realize the quality of faith you have and your life takes on exciting dimensions. When He lives in your heart and your thoughts, you will be able to face the future with peace and calmness. You will begin to see who you can become through God's strength, inspiration, and wisdom. Sadness can turn into joy, defeat into victory, fear disappears, hate changes to love, and despair to hope.

Pray to the Lord. Pray for the Lord to keep you in faith and to give you faith and strength to keep Him first in your life. As we pray, listen to what God says. He is our Lord who heals us. I love to stop and listen to God as He speaks to me. When I pray, I stop and get very quiet and still and listen.

I also take note of the angels God sends my way. Just like at the first of this book, how the man at Kmart (the angel) came up to me and told me what to do for my back and the girl I told you about that gave me the "Fear not for I am with you" bracelet, and remember the angel that gave me hope during the biopsy? How can anyone not believe in God?

He is so good. If you are not a believer, then you need to start praying and get a relationship with Him. You will always have someone to talk to, comfort you, support you, heal you, love you, be with you. He is the only one that can help you in a time of crisis. Your loved ones cannot do anything for you when you get an incurable disease, but God can. He works miracles. Have faith in Him and know He will be with you. Faith is a positive view of God and His ability to help us. Faith always expects something good to happen. We need faith. Without if we may be doubtful about the present and fearful of the future, which leads us into anxiety and depression. Look what He did for me.

With a transition, you will know God better. You will see His miracles working before you. The Holy Spirit will be with you to be good to people every day. If God calls us to do something that we think will be impossible, don't be afraid. He gives us power to do it. God's strength is made perfect in your weakness. Your life will be fulfilled with a deep inner peace. Your love and your relationship with your Lord will grow stronger. You will catch yourself praying and praising Him. God then becomes your communicator, your best friend, your Father, your protector, your supporter, your everything. God is faithful, and in His timing, He'll do it.

When you have God the center of your life, you will see that you desire God's presence in your life more than anything else. God will speak to you personally. You will feel His spirit and know when He has given you a gift. You will understand the Christian's language, the Bible, and you will obey God even more. God's promise is that you will have blessings. He will Bless you because He knows you. We grow in knowledge of Him and grow stronger in our spiritual growth.

Mama said that she might have Alzheimer's, but she will always know that God loves her, and she loves Him. That is one thing she will never forget. We do not know what the future holds for us or those we love. We too may get Alzheimer's as we age. But even then, the Lord will hold our hand and guide us through it like He holds Mama's hand. We cannot get away from His love and personal care even with Alzheimer's. Know that when trouble comes your way, you can have peace with the Lord.

I have found myself wanting to do for my children. Worrying about their problems and being sad when they are sad. We as parents want to handle the problems and struggles for our children, but God says, "When you release loved ones to Me, they are free to cling to My hand. As you entrust others into My care, I am free to shower blessings on them. My Presence will go with them wherever they go, and I will give them rest. This same presence stays with you, as you relax and place your trust in Me. Watch to see what I will do."

My daughter, Lisa, is very close to me. She had numerous challenges in her life. She has always believed in the Lord. While young, she was in church, and she went to a Christian school. As she grew up into adulthood, she has gone through some hardships. She has two children, who are precious. Her marriage was unstable at the time, so therefore, her financial situation was in a deep struggle.

The reason I am telling you about this is because I want you to know what happened in her situation that changed her life. There was a transformation in her life. She visited us at times being very depressed and unhappy. She had a big burden on her shoulders, trying to pay the bills and keeping above the water without drowning in debt. It was very overwhelming for her. My days were sad and stressful because her days were sad and stressful. She told me she could not figure out how to handle it.

My being a mom, I wanted to do whatever I could to help her, and in some ways her dad and I could, but mentally, she had to help herself or let God handle it. All we could do is pray to God for help. I prayed with her and said, "Lisa, you and I need to turn it over to the Lord and let Him handle it for us. Let go, let God."

One day, she prayed very hard from her heart. "Lord, I'm scared. I need your help."

All of a sudden, the Lord spoke to her and said, "Take one day at a time. I will be with you. Don't worry about yesterday or tomorrow. Know I will take care of you."

It clicked so hard and clear in her mind what the Lord said. She at that time was transformed in her mind. She at that time realized she was trying too hard to handle her problem herself. She could not do it. She needed to let God handle it. She had to turn it over to Him solely, and she did.

She came to me and said, "Mama, I don't worry anymore. I leave it to the Lord. I just think about today, not tomorrow or yesterday, and let Him lead me to where I need to be."

Her worrying diminished as her faith got stronger. She is a walking witness. She tells me all the time, "God is with me every step of the way. He knows my future, not I. He will lead, guide, and direct me through this. I have faith in His plan, in His timing, not mine." By her having peace of mind, it makes me have peace of mind.

She said, "I will be patient and wait on Him to give me the answers." God is showing her in all kinds of ways how He is looking out for her. For example, at Christmas, a friend came to her and said, "I ordered over three hundred dollars' worth of toys from Target, and they were delivered to my house. The next day, the same toys were delivered again to my house. I called Target and told them, and they said, "Just keep them." She then asked Lisa, "Would you like them for your children?"

"I thought of you because your children are a boy and a girl and the same age as mine."

My daughter was so excited. The toys were perfect for her children to have a wonderful Christmas.

Lisa said, "Mama, I always try to set up a budget and start the week out by holding to the side what I need and not what I want, and God always opened the door for what I needed."

She cried. "This is the Lord," she said. "I just know it."

These were just a few of the things God has shown her how He is looking out for her. He is constantly taking care of her. She is so happy now. She is doing better financially, but most of all, she has a piece of mind. She is not worrying and being sad like before, which makes her have a clearer mind to think and work. With her faith, it has been amazing to see all that has been restored in her life. Thank You, God, for taking care of her.

Transformation gives us the strength not only to endure the situation we face, but also to overcome them. My daughter now has a closer relationship with God. She told me that living for God is the greatest achievement you can accomplish in your life.

She prays constantly for the Lord's leading of her situation. She is more Christlike in her daily life. To do this, you have to grow spiritual to become like Jesus in the way we think, feel, and act. The more you develop Christlike character, the more you will bring glory to God. You cannot become Christlike on your own strength. Only the Holy spirit has the power to make the changes God wants to make in our lives. God is more interested in what you are than what you do.

Have a good attitude. Attitude is so important in a transformation. Anyone can go through a difficult time with a bad attitude; it takes a Christlike attitude to endure it victoriously. You will think differently about yourself and about the people around you. Being Christlike is not being selfish. We need to change our thinking to be like God's. We need to rely on Christ's strength, not our strength. God wants us to put ourselves in the shoes of others and allowing our hearts to feel compassion; we can help those who are hurting. We need to have patience. At the right time, the Holy Spirit will give us the words to say. It is thinking of other's instead of ourselves. God will make you what you ought to be. He will strengthen you and make you secure. He will work in you to become the person He plans for you to be. God knows what you need. He will provide to you.

Transformation renews your mind to God's attitude. Our thinking contains a lot of power. If we dwell on the negative, then we have a negative attitude, which makes everyone become negative around you, and it makes you more negative. Being negative is not from God. It's from the devil. If you think God's thoughts, God's thoughts will fill you with faith and strength, which will make you have positive thoughts, and you will be in line with God's Word.

We all face challenges. We think God is punishing us. God has a purpose for all things that come to strengthen our faith and grow strong. Be patient and calm and know that God will turn your struggles into victory. God will bring good out of the situation. He can turn all situations around. I look down at my bracelet constantly and read, "Fear not for I am with you." This gives me assurance you are with me Lord. Faith is all that can get me through this. I myself do not know where to go or what to do, but through your faith I do get through this.

"Therefore, if anyone is in Christ, he is a new creation; the old has gone, the new has come!" (2 Corinthians 5:17). Are you reflecting Jesus in your life? Ask God to transform you.

He has promised, "You shall serve the Lord your God and He will take sickness from the mist of you" (Exodus 23:25) because He promised, "I am the Lord who heals you" (Exodus 15:26). God's Word says He held all your diseases (Psalm 103:3). Jesus Christ has redeemed me from diseases because He "Himself took infirmities and bore your sickness" (Matthew 8:17) at the whipping post (Matthew 27:26, John 19:1), "and therefore, by His stripes, you were healed" (Peter 2:24). My sickness and pain began to vanish; my weakness was then transformed into strength. Today is a new day, a fresh start (Lamentations 3:23).

"In addition to all, taking up the shield of faith with which you will be able to extinguish all the flaming arrows of the evil one" (Ephesians 6:16).

First Corinthians 15:49. God's will is that every Christian might be conformed to the image of His son. If you are sick and weak and feel like it's more than you can bear, just know the facts. He cares for you; He will cleanse you. Be assured He knows when the work is done. He wants you to be in His image. I never knew my daddy to worry. He would get upset, but he would forget about it and not worry about it.

It is easy to get discouraged. You may feel that life is not fair, but God is still guiding you. When you pray and have a relationship with the Lord, He will work your harm to your advantage. If you're not faithful, then you will always wonder if you are going to be harmed, but if you are faithful and trust Him, then God will lead you in the right direction. You will always be blessed.

It's easy to trust Him when things are going good, but you have to learn to trust Him when things are not going good. We either choose to be negative and live discouraged, or we stay positive and let

God show you what He can do. Mama told me one time, "The rain will come, but the sun will shine soon." I've always thought of that when I get sick or have problems. The rain is only temporary. A cure may seem impossible, but God can do the impossible. Keep a good attitude. Be encouraged. You will see God will take you to a better place, a better health report, and a better life.

Let go, let God. Do not waiver your faith at hard times. His promise to you is that all things work together for good (Romans 8:28). This means something good will come out of even your greatest tragedy. God's love, grace, and mercy assures us that even though we endure deep sorrow, joy comes in the morning (Psalms 30:5). Our disappointments, losses, and failures don't have to destroy our future. When you worship God for who He is and thank Him for His great plan in your situation, you will see His glory revealed as He brings good out of it.

Let go, let God. Make sure you do not let your mind go back to the devil. The devil can enter your mind and mess up your life. People who walk with a leading from the Lord have a sense of purpose. When we walk step-by-step with God through each crisis, we will see Him do a miraculous work of transforming, restoring, and healing. If you pray and have a close relationship and are humble and have a faith-filled heart, you will see God's goodness in the midst of all that's happening to you. Ask God to be in charge of your life. Once you do, leave it in His hands. Let go, let God. Daddy always said to me, "Don't worry. Be happy." You have to let go, let God.

Have a close relationship with God by letting Him handle your problems. You will see His miracles working before you. You will want to know Him more. The Holy Spirit will be with you to be good to people every day. If God calls us to do something that we think will be impossible, don't be afraid. He gives us power to do it. God's strength is made perfect in your weakness. God will help you to think the right thoughts and actions during a transition.

Right actions equal new habits, which change your character, and God will lead you into a better, calmer, and happier person. Be excited to face the day. Enjoy every challenge you face by knowing God will be with you to guide you in the right path. Enjoy your life.

Slow down and ask God for wisdom and listen for His guidance. Take time and see if you have peace.

Listen to God. Sometimes you have to get to the other side of a circumstance to see the whole picture of what God is doing in your life. God may be trying to separate you from some situation that is keeping you from receiving the better plan He has for you. He may be encouraging better health for you.

Lisa called me a few days ago, and she told me something else the Lord has done for her that was amazing. She said she had a problem that came up, and she went to the Lord with it. She prayed, "Lord, my doors are open for You to come in. Give me what I need to do."

She said to me, "Mama, it is amazing where He carries me. If I had not prayed for His guidance, I would have handled it myself, and I could have never did a great job like He did." A deep inner peace comes from God. When trouble comes, peace comes when you get God's prospective on your troubles.

This is why we should always go to the Lord in prayer and listen to Him with our problems. Be willing to obey God, even if you don't understand what He is doing with you. Do everything you can to keep peace and enjoy your life. Just listen for God's voice. When we walk in obedience with Him, we don't miss His direction for our lives. When we obey God, we see answers to our prayers because He will lead us.

Prayer

Lord, there are times when I feel pulled in
other directions that may not be pleasing to You.
Give me grace and strength to keep You first in
my life.

Let God increase your faith. We learn important lessons about God in our life experiences. We grow in knowledge of Him and grow stronger in our spiritual growth. Pray to receive God's power of transformation, and God will change you. Once you do this, go about your normal day. Expect His leading. If you listen to His voice, He will lead, guide, and direct you.

Don't worry. He will transform you. Worry is focused thinking on something negative. Meditate and pray, which is focusing on God's Word instead of your problems. When you know the Lord is guiding and taking care of you, everyday life becomes exciting. Make sure you don't let your mind go back to the enemy. Leave unresolved circumstances in God's hands. Ask God for courage to go forward.

The devil can enter your mind and mess up your life. Even with circumstances that you feel the devil is stealing your peace and joy say, "Devil, you are not going to steal this from me." Satan is not after your joy; he is after your strength. He wants you weak, too weak to be happy and too weak to pray. Put your trust in God, and He will shield you from your enemy. Grow in wisdom. Have faith. Faith is having peace when you don't know the answer (2 Samuel 22:31).

God is our hope, our peace, our strength, and our joy. He is the only one we can put our faith in. Trust in His power, wisdom, and goodness.

Praise and worship is the means by which God transforms our lives. God is secure in the knowledge of His greatness, power, and perfection. We are the ones who forget. We need to show Him that we know who He is. God intends worship to restore, motivate, fulfill, and bless us. Our greatest blessing comes when we take the focus off ourselves and put in entirely on God in worship and praise. There are times in our life, like mine, that praise and worship are the only things you can do in situations.

You praise God while struggles surround you. This is what will definitely change your life if it hasn't yet. Just know that worship is our choice. If we don't make the choice, then we cannot make it a way of life, and if we don't make praise a way of life, we will never experience all God has for us. It's your own personal worship times that you will develop a relationship with Him.

If you worship God and you do not sense His presence, continue to praise and worship until you do. Soon you will hear God speak to you. You will experience His love, and He will change your emotions, attitude, and patterns of thought. He will make your mind clear to better understand His Word. He will refresh, fulfill, renew, enrich, and He will heal you and give you His power and joy. He will redeem and transform you. He will take you out of fear and doubt and give you peace. He will lift you above your circumstances.

"Be careful [anxious] for nothing; but in everything by prayer" (Philippians 4:6–7). "Whatever you desire when you pray, believe that you will receive it, and you shall have it" (Mark 11:24).

"Nothing can ever separate us from God's love. Death can't, and life can't. Our fears for today, our worries about tomorrow" (Romans 8:38–39). Hair loss can't. Chemotherapy can't. Radiation can't. A bad diagnosis can't. Our symptoms of nausea and even the frustration of late lab results can't keep God's love away. Whether our blood counts are high or low, nothing in our cancer experience will ever be able to separate us from the love of God. Do you feel far from God's love? He's right beside you. Ask Him to help you.

"And do not be conformed to this world, but be transformed by the renewing of your mind, so that you may prove what the will of God is, that which is good and acceptable and perfect" (Romans 12:2). God's Word says not to be conformed to the world's ways but to be transformed by renewing our minds.

Matthew 7:11. Blessings received shows us about His mercy and goodness

"The Lord is near to those who have a broken heart" (Psalm 34:18). If we allow God's work to be done in us, we might be surprised at what He can do through us.

Psalm 37:1–11, Jeremiah 13:13. God takes away the bitterness in your life and gives sweetness in its place.

Chapter 25

WHEN ONE DOOR CLOSES, ANOTHER DOOR OPENS

I will tell you about the story of my husband's success by always pushing for his dream through faith. Success comes from having dreams and goals to go forward. Gary had a dream, and with his faith and trust in God, he went for it. That is why he is successful today. He is all about helping his family, coworkers, friends, and strangers. He is the rock of our whole family and cares about everyone's happiness and well-being.

While young, he always felt he had to prove himself with everything. When he was one year old, his mom and dad divorced. His mom had custody of him. She remarried when he was two, and he never really knew his paternal dad till years later after he married me. His stepfather was a wonderful father. He made him feel loved and appreciated. This meant so much for him to have him as a father growing up. He was a blessing in his life.

Gary's mom had another son, Rex, a few years later by his stepfather. His stepdad treated his paternal son, Rex, no different from him. He still felt love from him.

Gary was a hard worker on the farm. He lived in the house with his mom, brother, stepdad, and her parents. When he was in high school, he drove a bus and came home and worked till dark on their farm. He worked in cotton, tobacco, and livestock. Every Sunday, they were in church.

In 1968, Gary and I met. We were married in 1969. He worked at Lundy Packing Company, buying hogs and cleaning out their pens. It was a nasty job. He was making $2 an hour. In July 1970, he and I had a baby girl. We named her Lisa Kay Porter. She was beautiful and a miracle from God.

In August 1971, he got an opportunity to go to work at a tire company. He was starting out with $450 a month working in the Chemical Lab. After a few years, he was making $500 a month. We were so excited. This was a lot of salary back then.

In 1971, we bought a ten-by-fifty-two house trailer and one and a half acres of land closer to Gary's work. In November 1971, we had a precious baby boy, Steve Clanton Porter. He was premature and had to stay in an incubator for a few months before he could come home. In no time, he was a healthy baby.

In 1976, he and I bought a thirty-acre farm with an old house on it. We found out later that the old house was a house my grandmother's sister lived in back in the early 1900s. We were shocked. We had no idea when we bought it. We moved the old house to the side of the farm, and we bought a new house trailer, twelve by sixty-five. We felt so blessed. We had three bedrooms instead of two and two bathrooms instead of one. We made it our home, and we were very happy. It was a struggle keeping up the mortgage payments, so we had to bring in extra income.

The land was a hay farm, which we worked putting up hay and selling hay to others. We chopped and sold wood and raised livestock on the farm. He would work a full-time job at Kelly-Springfield and come home and work till dark. Our children would go to school every day and come home and work till dark. They would help their dad chop wood and put up hay in the barn. I had a home-cooked meal when they came in to eat at dark. They worked hard. I worked as a teacher's assistant at their school so I could get off from work when they did. I had the afternoons and the summer off with them.

I think back how Gary started out working for someone else, cleaning their hogpens and buying their hogs, and now, he is the one raising the hogs and selling them himself. We felt so blessed that he had gone this far. We built a house on the property in 1978. It was beautiful. We were so proud of it.

He got a promotion as an engineer after working at the tire company for years and doing a great job. He was doing the same job as the engineers that worked in his department did. The employer said he deserved it. They gave him a promotion even though he did not have a degree in college for it.

It was in the 1980s. He had worked at this tire company for seventeen years. He was a model employee, but he was limited in his opportunities for growth in this business. He felt if he got the opportunity to find something that he would like better, he was going after it.

He has always been a person to keep looking for new adventures and opportunities. At times we can get in the valley, and we are scared to climb up the mountain. He is one that will never give up, and he will try to climb to the top to see what is there!

Gary's dream was to own an auto dealership. He even named it. He said he was going to name it "Vern's Used Cars and Trucks." My brother-in-law told him not to stand still if he wanted to go further. He told him about an opportunity to go to work at a dealership in Overland Park, Kansas. Dave was the man that was the general manager there, and he said he would hire him.

He did not know if he could even sell cars, but in his thinking, he was so excited. It was like someone was saying, "Gary, go for it." Even though he had no training or experience, taking the big step to move to Kansas and get in car business was a huge step. It not only would change his life; it would change ours. He felt like this was an opportunity to work toward getting his dream dealership one day—"Vern's Used Cars and Trucks."

When God gives you a dream, you will know it. There will be oppositions, delays, adversities, and things you don't understand. You will get discouraged and think it is never going to happen. The enemy will try to stop you reaching your new levels. He knows you are following the steps of faith and setting a new standard. He knows there is nothing he can do to stop you, but he will try to persuade you to settle where you are. He will give you negative thoughts. This is all part of the process you will go through. When you feel fear, it is Satan trying to discourage you from your dream. You can come out bitter or you can come out better. God didn't bring Gary this far to leave him. He doesn't send difficulty or problems, but He will use it. You have a tendency to trust God in the good times, and you need to trust Him in the difficult times also.

God uses problems to direct us, correct us, and protect us. Don't push your dreams away. Make it alive. It will strengthen you.

Gary knew he needed to keep pushing forward in his faith and do his part to reach his dream. When it all comes together, it will work out for the good. He and I talked about the job opportunity for a couple of weeks. Wow! What a move!

At times, we let the fear of the unknown hold us back from this opportunity. You don't know about the unknown or whether this is the right move or not. We were questioning ourselves as to whether we are going to financially be able to make it or not. Gary said he felt as if the Lord was giving him this opportunity to go forward at this time of his life. When we are left to work out matters ourselves, we go to the Lord. We knew that problems can be opportunities, and sometimes God allows opportunities to come our way to help us grow and mature. We have to pray about it and let God lead us in the right direction. He knows the future and what is in our heart. God has a plan for us in His timing. His plan is bigger than our plan.

We were in a challenging situation. We caught ourselves saying, "What if this doesn't work out? What if I don't like it? What if they don't like me?" We need to keep our strength, pray, and let God carry us through it. We know there will be ups and downs, twist and turns, and disappointments. We know that it is up to us as to what our outcome will be.

He was in his midthirties, and he knew if he was going to make a change, it had to be now. He wanted to see if there is something else out there for him that would be more challenging and goal oriented than what he was doing. At the time, Gary couldn't see it, but God did. He trusted God and stayed in faith.

People at times lose sight of going for their dreams because they feel trapped in their circumstances. They have a hard time looking beyond their limits. They don't see how they can make a change. They are scared and have fear. You have to build your confidence and move forward to make it happen. Step in the unknown, and you will see miracles. Life has a way of pushing our dreams down.

As I said before, Gary and I prayed together. Two are better than one. God, it is in Your hands. We trust You even when we don't understand what we are doing. We decided together to go for it. We had to sale our farm and house. We turned it over to a real estate company. It took a while to sell our farm. We sold it, and the children had a couple months of school left, so he went to Kansas, and I stayed at my parents till they got out of school and we could find a place to rent in Kansas.

In the meanwhile, he got a flight to Overland Park, Kansas, and reserved a hotel room to stay in till he could get something permanent when we came there. When he arrived in the hotel room, he was unpacking his clothes, and he saw a note that I hid in his suitcase, giving him words of encouragement and telling him the children and I are proud of him and love him.

He walked to the window and looked out. It was snowing. Everything looked so strange. He went from working at a company of seventeen years as an engineer making a good salary and going to a small dealership making no salary, just commission only on what he sold. He knew he needed to give it his best and have an excellent attitude and spirit, but he was sad and scared and said, "Lord, what have I done?"

God spoke to him, "Be a warrior to reach your full potential. If you step into the unknown, you will see miracles. The door will close, and it is up to you to push it. A push down can be a push up. A closed door means a new door will open. The right people will show up. The only thing that can stop you is you. You will be out of your comfort zone for a while, but trust Me. You will face challenges. You have too much potential to get stuck in the valley. You can restore double what you lost. Remember the dream you have and go to the top of the mountain with it."

Gary said, "I've come this far with the Lord beside me, and He want let me down now. I have to refocus and go for it with all I have."

The dealership opened the next morning, and he was the first one there. Dave was the manager. He introduced himself; He had talked to him on the telephone several times earlier and felt like he already knew him. Dave was very kind.

He spent time with him, showing him around and introducing him to other employees. Everyone liked Gary. They liked his southern accent. God was growing him up.

When he got the job, he went full blast with it. He was at the dealership every morning when the doors opened, and he was the last one to leave at night. By having the southern voice, he was able to break the ice with customers, and they loved him. He got top sales most months.

At the time, I was working helping out with the payments and keeping the children in school. The children and I moved to Kansas in a rented house Gary and Dave found for us. We were excited, but it was many miles from my family. I missed them so much.

A year later, Gary found out that he and Dave were going to be transferred to Charlotte, North Carolina, with a new dealership. We were so excited. Now I could go back to my home place and be close to family. The children and I moved to Charlotte while Dave and Gary could get everything settled in Kansas to move.

When we moved to Charlotte, I put the kids in a public school. They came home every day, saying they did not like it. I called Gary and said, "We have got to put them in another school, no matter what."

After I told him how the children came home upset every day. He said, "Just do it. The Lord will get us through this."

The next day, I took them to a Christian school and had them enrolled, not knowing how we were going to afford it. The first day, my daughter came home and told me her teacher told her they needed someone in the business office. I went the next day and applied, and I got the job. They paid me a salary, plus they paid for the tuition for both of the children. I could not believe it. I loved the job and ended up working there ten years. God, You did it! Thank You for Your miracles You give us!"

Gary moved to Charlotte, and we bought a house. So excited! He worked at the new dealership, getting it ready to open. We were happy to be able to settle down in our new home, and I was close to my family, which made me even happier.

A year later, the owner's business went under. Gary was panicking. He had no job all of a sudden, and then Hugo the hurricane came through. He now had no job. Trees were blown down all around us, and we could not even get on the streets, for trees were blocking cars. We had no electricity and no water.

Gary was panicking again. There was no way to get out and find a job, two children in school, and a new mortgage payment. We found out that Dave was also blocked in with trees. He lived down the street, so he went to help him. We were in the house nine days. No way to get groceries. Everything was shut down. No job and no way to get out to look for a job.

Gary finally got where he could get out, but there still was no water. He had to go out while it was raining and take a shower with his bathing suit on while the water running out of the gutter. He went to the BMW store, and they hired him. He loved working at the BMW store. Dave went to work at the Pontiac store. Dave called him and wanted him to work with him, and he went because he felt Dave needed him, and he owed him.

After he started to work at the Pontiac store, a new manager took over at the Hendrick BMW store and fired everyone working there. He knew then the Lord was with him not to stay there. That was the Lord still carrying him forward to his dream.

The Hendrick Pontiac store was going under and not doing good. Gary and Dave worked hard to get it stronger. In the meanwhile, Rick Hendrick called Gary and Dave and wanted them to meet with him, and they did. Hendrick had bought a new Saturn franchise, and he wanted Gary to work full-time at the Saturn store to start up the new car Saturn dealership. He asked Dave to stay at the Pontiac store and oversee the Saturn store. They accepted it, and he went to work at Saturn.

Saturn was new, and customers had to check it out, but in one week, five or six hundred customers came in, and they didn't sell a car. Later, Saturn started selling, and we were so excited. Saturn was a good car, and its gross was good. They took care of their customers and the business was growing. Gary with Saturn only and Dave with the Pontiac store and overseeing the Saturn store worked there for years. Thank you, Dave, for your support.

In the year 2000, Hendrick sold out the Saturn dealership. That meant that Gary would be working for someone else. He still had to keep his trust in the Lord that the right person would come and buy the dealership that he would like. The Lord brought this man named Bill and his wife, Wanda, into our life. He asked Gary if he would go in with him as a partner and buy the Saturn dealership. He wanted him to keep working there. He knew that God brought Bill to him.

Gary was finally getting his dream. He was offered to buy a dealership with an honest person who had the knowledge of car sales, financing, and insurance and could help him conquer his dream. He was so happy to accept. Gary and his partner bought the Saturn franchise. They were so excited. They worked very good together as a team. They then adventured out and bought another Saturn dealership and then a third and fourth dealership. Things were going so good.

Steve, our son, went to work with Saturn to help his dad. He was working with Honda, which he loved, but knew his dad needed him. Steve was the general manager of two of the stores. Gary is happy to have his son working with him. I am so blessed to have my husband and my son working together.

In the year 2009, I found out I had lung cancer, and they only gave me three months to live. Help! We prayed together, and we were scared. I started taking chemo. Then I went through surgery and radiation. Lord, help us. Where can we turn? We did not have anyone to turn to but the Lord.

While I was going through the medical procedures of cancer, Gary and I found out that the Saturn cars were no longer being made through the Saturn manufacturing company, which meant there are no cars made to be sold. Lord, this cannot be happening to us. My son worked with several of the stores, and he was going to be affected by this also. I just found out I have cancer, and Gary, his partner, and my son were without a job.

Gary and his partner had four dealership buildings empty with no new cars to sell. This was a nightmare. We prayed, "Lord, be with us through this."

We knew at times you have to go through the bad times to get to the good times. You may have to struggle, but trust in God, and He will show you His plan in the long run. We have to keep growing and not let fear hold us back. We have to stay focused and grow stronger every day as situations come before us. We will not get discouraged. We know God is in control, but this was too much to comprehend. We know life is hard, but this was so much to have at one time. We are not supposed to question the Lord, but I wanted to say, "Why, Lord? Why us?" We knew we have to move forward and stay open-minded. We knew our faith in God will take care of us, but this felt like the end was coming.

I had lung cancer. Gary and Bill's dream was gone. Steve, our son, was without a job. I started thinking negative thoughts: *This can't be happening. Why, Lord.* I knew then I had to go forward with my thinking and not be negative, so I prayed and prayed from my heart, "Lord, please help us." I had to let go and let God.

Mama always told me, "Brenda, it may be raining now, but the sun will shine again." My mom has always been an angel on earth, and there are so many quotes she made in my life that stood out, and that was one of them. My daddy also gave me good advice; he would say, "Brenda, it'll come back. Don't worry. Know that without the rain, you can't grow."

God gave me good doctors, and I went through chemo, surgery, and radiation. God was good. I tried to be strong for Gary and myself to get through this. I gave it to God, and God blessed me. As time was passing, with the Lord's help, I fought hard and beat the cancer.

God was with Gary during this time. He was still preparing him to go for his dream even though we were going through all these obstacles. A lot of people let frustrations cause them to get mad, lose their passion, and slack off. What he was facing was a test. If he was not doing the right thing, then God could not lead him to where he is supposed to be. Gary gave it to God, and God blessed him. God would not have allowed this to happen if He wasn't going to bring good out of it. He has your best interest at heart. It's a part of His plan. God had another plan for Gary. He had something else for him to do. We could not see it at the time because we do not know the unknown.

God could see things in Gary that he could not see himself. His plan for his life was bigger than his plan. His plan for my life was to live and witness for Him, and that is why I am writing this book. I will always witness and let everyone know He is the reason I am here today. Thank You, Jesus.

Gary had already gone through times of disappointments. He had a dream and things were going sideways. He would take a step forward, and then it became a step backward. I was going through cancer, and now another failure with his company closing down that supplied them with their cars to sell.

The journey is more important than the destination because if you don't learn what's prepared for you in the journey, you won't be able to handle where God is taking you. God will take you to new opportunities that will be what is the best for you in the future. God says, "Keep going! I'm in control." God is fighting your battles. You may not see this, but don't give up. God is there for you. Your hope is in Him.

Gary's partner Bill called him and said, "We have an opportunity to buy franchises to go into our four buildings and property." He had figured out that the manufacturing company for several different franchises could help us.

Gary was so happy that they had another chance to go for it. He said, "Yes, let's go for it," and they did.

Pushing forward and never giving up—and with God's help— all things worked out good. Gary did not make it happen with his strength alone. He made it happen step by step with faith. God worked out His plan for our life through our faith and being patient in His timing. We went through several dark places, but the Lord gave us our dream.

Gary and Bill are partners and are very blessed with the performance of the dealerships. A setback can be a setup for a comeback if you keep having the faith and pushing toward it. With the good Lord's help, He paved our way for Gary to get his dream dealerships.

God brought Bill, his partner, into our lives to help make it happen. A special thank you to Bill, Wanda, Steve, Bonnie, and all the wonderful employees who have supported us through the years. God took Gary and me to where we had never dreamed.

Thank You, Jesus, for being with us during all the difficult times that we went through to get to where we are today. You have made us stronger and helped us know that You are always with us in our hard times as well as our good times. You know what's best for us, and we trust You. We will follow Your direction in all that we do. Amen.

When we look back on our life, we can see things so clear. It took going through all the twist and turns to get where we are today. Years later, we saw the reality of it. Now we can see that God had a plan for us and was guiding our steps through it all. We thought at times we were going backward, but God was setting us up to move forward in His timing. Gary said, "God allowed me to have the courage to go to Kansas to start a new future, and the same God that allowed this is the one that took me through it." It took his faith to keep pushing, and he did, and that is why we are where we are today.

As of today, I have no cancer. Gary and Bill are working together, and things are prospering with the new dealerships. Our son is working and happy. Things are going good. Life is great. We know there can always be difficulties in the future, but we have to keep our faith that He is always there for us and working His plan out, not ours.

Gary stepped into a new opportunity with a new level in his life. God can shut the doors to open new ones, and by taking a step of faith, you can push yourself into your destiny. The new adventure did not defeat him; it promoted him!

The opportunities he went through helped him grow and was the best thing he could have done. If he had stayed still, it would have stunted his growth. He would not be where he is today.

- Pray and ask for His guidance. He will give you great blessings. Thank You, Jesus, for your blessings in our life.
- God will work His plan for you. You don't have to. He knows the best direction to take you.

- The God who gave you the dream in your thoughts is the same God who will conquer your dream. God will finish what He started. His plan will be fulfilled for you.
- Don't settle in the valley. Climb to the top of the mountain, and you will have a blessing.
- Setbacks can be a set up for a comeback.
- In all your ways know, recognize, and acknowledge Him, and He will direct and make your paths straight and plain.

I'm too blessed to be stressed and too anointed to be disappointed.

I refuse to be discouraged, to be sad or cry. I refuse to be downhearted, and here's the reason why:

I have God who is almighty; who is sovereign and supreme;

I have a God who loves me, and I am on his team.

He is all wise and powerful; Jesus is His name!

Though everything else is changeable, my God remains the same!

I refuse to be defeated. My eyes are on my God.

He has promised to be with me, as through this life I trod.

I am looking past my circumstances, to heaven's throne above. My prayers have reached the heart of God. I am resting in his love.

I give thanks to Him in everything. My eyes are on His face.

The battle is His; the victory is mine; He will help me win the race. I'm so blessed to be stressed.

On my bad days, I seek you. On my good days, I thank You. On my great days, I praise You. But every day, I need You!

Happy Moments—Praise God. Difficult Moments—Seek God. Quiet Moments—Worship God. Painful Moments—Trust God. Every Moment—Thank God.

If we fill our hours with regrets over the failure of yesterday and with worries over the problems of tomorrow, we have no today in which to be thankful.

Yesterday was a dream and tomorrow a vision.

But today, well lived, makes every yesterday a dream of happiness and every tomorrow a vision of hope.

"After you have followed in his footsteps, He will restore, support and strengthen you. He will place you on a firm foundation" (1 Peter 5:10).

Isaiah: God's ways are higher than our ways, and His plans are better than our plans. God is in control.

"The Lord will work out His plans for my life" (Psalm 138). "Lean on trust in, and be confident in the Lord with all your heart and mind and do not rely on your own insight or understanding" (Proverbs 3:5–7 AMPC).

"In the day when I called, you answered me; and you strengthened me with strength in my inner self" (Psalm 138:3 AMPC).

Chapter 26

Satan Does Not Conquer

By your faith, you know that Satan cannot lay a disease on your body because Christ has already borne your disease for you. You rebuke Satan with the Word of God in the name of Jesus. Have no fear.

Jesus says, "When sickness and disease begin to appear," Satan is desiring to destroy your health, but God will be with you. He has promised, "You shall serve the Lord your God, and He will take sickness away from the midst of you" (Exodus 23:25). "I am the Lord who heals you" (Exodus 15:26). God's Word says, "He heals all your diseases" (Psalm 103:3). "By His stripes you were healed" (1 Peter 2:24).

The Bible says in John 10:10 that it is Satan that is the enemy who comes to steal, kill, and destroy. Jesus came that we might have life abundantly.

Trust God. Storms may come, winds may blow, enemies may attack, Satan may oppose, circumstance may seem impossible, but God says, "I'll stand by you. I'll never forsake you. You shall never perish."

God doesn't promise an easy life. He said, "In this world you will have tribulations." Tribulations cannot overcome us. Trials cannot defeat us and hell cannot destroy us. We know all things work together for good to them that love God (Romans 8:28).

When the road of life's journey gets rough, God is always there, reaching out to help us. God uses problem circumstances to draw us closer to Him. Jesus warned there will be problems in the world. Life is a series of problems. Your most intimate experiences of worship will most likely be in your darkest days. Problems force us to go to God and depend on Him instead of ourselves. You will see yourself turning to God alone. When we learn to trust Him and reach out to Him by faith, we find the path easier to walk.

Never give up. Have faith that God knows what is best for us in our life. We choose to do the right thing and then trust God's spirit to give us His power, love, faith, and wisdom to do it. Since God's spirit lives in us, these things are always available for the asking. Know that God is going through the problems with us. God will never leave us on our own.

Trust His love in spite of our circumstances. God is in control. God was in my crisis and still is. I trust that He is with me now and always in my time of need. With Him, the only direction I now want is to reach up and take His hand and never let go. His desire is that I become more dependent upon Him for every step I make. He wants to take me places I have never been. In order to do that, I have to go through the low valleys of life, places where I could easily get lost or off track.

"God is still on the throne. He always cares for His own. His promise is true; He will not forget you, God is still on the throne" (author unknown). Don't waiver in your faith with God. Keep your attitude of faith. No one can have faith for you. Others can pray for you, but you have to have faith for yourself. You cannot depend on someone else keeping you happy. You must make a decision to be a believer. Be positive, believe, and have faith in God. Your faith helps overcome bad obstacles. Focus on God and not you. Stop thoughts of what you cannot do and start thoughts of what God can do for you, and believe He will do it for you.

You have an individual right to pray for and receive every blessing promised. Pray and leave the results with Him. Your prayer will be answered to the fullest extent, for God will say to you, "Go your way, and as you have believed, so be it done to you." In the scripture of Matthew 8:13, God's promises are for you personally. Have faith and stand up for the Word of God.

Prayer

> God, please teach me Your ways and help
> me to become closer to Thee.

Unbeliever's may say, "I am out of control. I feel so helpless with all this stress in my life." But by having a relationship with God, you will be a believer.

Believer's say, "God is with me. He will take care of me. I am grateful to God for my strength." We want our situations to change, but nothing will change in our lives without having God in our life, spiritually, mentally, and physically. Change comes through prayers and then through waiting patiently on God for His timing, plan, and purpose. While we are waiting for God to solve our problems, we need to stay positive. God tells us to trust Him. He rescues us from our troubles. Whatever we are struggling with today, the Holy Spirit will help you live a self-controlled life because the Bible says this in Galatians 5:22–23. We need to allow the Holy Spirit to help us admit when we need His help. Ask God for help from the Holy Spirit. God is in control.

Draw strength from God by exercising your faith and doing what He tells you to do. All good and perfect gifts come from God (James 1:17).

There are two kinds of faith, a delivering faith and a sustaining faith. Delivering faith is when God instantly turns your situation around. When that happens, it's great. But it takes a greater faith and a deeper walk with God to have that sustaining faith. That's when circumstances don't change immediately, but you say, "God, I don't care what comes against me. I don't care how long it takes. This thing is not going to defeat me. It's not going to get me down. I know You are on my side. And as long as You are for me, that's all that matters."

Sustaining faith is what gets you through those dark nights when you don't know where to go or what to do, and it seems you can't last another day, but because of your faith in God, you do. When you have that kind of attitude, the devil doesn't have a chance with you.

Besides, it's not usually the devil that causes our problems; it's how we respond to the devil. You can have a little problem, and it can defeat you, but on the other hand, you can have a huge problem, and you can be happy and at peace. This is an attitude of faith. They are believing for things to change. They are determined to live in victory. When you face struggles, you need to remind yourself that whatever is trying to defeat you could very well be what God will use to promote you.

Do not give up. Be strong and keep your, faith which will give you hope. Don't give up or be discouraged. God is with you. It will destroy hope. Without hope, we give up, which is what the devil wants us to do. Be positive. Positive minds produce positive lives; negative minds produce negative lives. They are always full of fear and doubt. Satan wants to attack our minds by overloading it with negative thoughts. The mind should be kept peaceful and alert. God wants to lift us up.

The devil wants to do the opposite. The devil uses anxiety and worry to attack our mind to distract us from serving Him. He uses this to press our faith down so it cannot rise up and help us have a stress-free life. Trust for a well body and believe that you will recover. He wants you to be a conqueror and rebuke sickness and disease. You cannot walk in victory if you are depending on someone else's faith. You must personally believe in the Lord as your Savior, and then you will be saved.

You must hear the Word of God. You must believe in the Lord as your healer. Then "by His stripes," you are healed. To be healed, you have the right to do your own asking, believing, claiming, and receiving, and you will be healed. To be saved, you do your own repenting, believing, confessing, accepting, and receiving, and then you are saved.

Don't let the devil steal your joy and peace. Satan is not after your joy; he is after your strength and peace. If he gets your peace, then he got your joy, which takes away from your strength to get through your setbacks in life. Be strong and resist his temptations that will make you worry. Say the word Jesus all through the day because the devil hates that name. If you feel like your peace and joy are slipping away, talk to the devil; say, "Forget it, devil. You are not getting me upset today!"

Don't talk to yourself, saying, "I just can't take any more of this." Instead, talk back to the devil as Jesus did (Luke 4:1–13). The Lord is my strength. Being happy makes me strong, and being mad or sad makes me weak.

Don't have negative thoughts. Satan tries to capture our thoughts early in the morning. He wants us to think about all the wrong things as we wake up. This intent is to steal our peace by upsetting us early in the morning. We need to defeat the devil early each day. Praise God and pray to Him as soon as our eyes open to a new day. Seek God's direction in the morning to gather His daily words for you. We need to obey and wait on God's timing because God's help will strengthen us to behave in a godly way if we trust in Him. We need to be strengthened mentally, physically, and emotionally. Be strong so you will not fall apart every time you face a situation not planned on.

Know that God is love. Sickness and disease are not of love. Disease steals health and happiness. It fills us with anxiety, pain, doubt, fear, and robs us of faith. Disease is not the will of God. It is the will of Satan. Jesus healed the sick (Acts 10:38). To believe this means they are deceived by Satan. God said, "I am the Lord who heals you" (Exodus 15:26).

Read God's Word. Feed on His Word and live in His Word, and you will produce faith in your heart. It cannot be seen, heard, or felt with your eyes and ears. The Bible says, "We walk by faith, not by sight" (2 Corinthians 5:7). "Without faith, it is impossible to please God" (Hebrews 11:6). God wants you to know that you have power over the devil and sickness.

Read the Word of God. The Bible is the truth. The Bible is God's Word. God hears you when you read His Word and pray to Him. You will become closer to Him by having a relationship with Him. You will recognize when Satan is talking to you, and you will know to ignore him and go to the Lord. When you have a relationship with God, He listens to your needs and can work miracles on your health.

Put your confidence in Him and His Word. When I first found out about my cancer, I first felt betrayed by God. I was miserable and unhappy. It was poisoning me. I read once, "Difficulties can plant seeds and once the weeds start growing, it wants to take over, chocking out all beauty." It affects not only you but everyone around you. Your mind can be an uproar. The devil loves taking our confidence from us. He wants us to feel like a failure.

While going through my rough times, I had to keep my faith. The devil would put doubts in my mind, but by reading Psalm 46:10, I knew I could have confidence that whatever happened, God would be in the midst of it all. I never felt abandoned by God. God see's my tears, and He knows my fears. Trials in our time will appear, but they don't have the power to control us when our faith resist God. We need to say, "I can do all things through Christ who strengthens me."

The devil attacks our confidence by convincing us that we will never change. He plants negative thoughts in our mind. You cannot be happy and bitter at the same time. Bitterness poisons everything in those who hold it. It troubles the mind. There is a lady I knew that was very bitter at the world. She constantly thought of ways to cause problems. She was very negative and bitter at the world and everyone around her. She didn't have an open heart to listen to the Word. She knew everything. She did not have a believing heart. I wish I could have helped her. She has to help herself. No one wants to be around her.

Why do people choose to be this way? It's the devil. Do not allow the devil to take over you. Have a believing and faithful heart. Let God and God's Word enter you and change. This person is very unhappy with herself and everyone and everything in life.

If you are a person with bitterness, think about the harm you do to your family and friends. You are pushing them away. The cure for complaining is to shift our focus from ourselves to others and to God. We have to handle it ourselves. He is faithful to complete His work in us when we turn over our lives completely to Him. Have faith because it allows us to see life from God's prospective. We will love ourselves and others and through this other's will love us.

Galatians 5:22–23. God desires to fill us with peace, joy, love, patience, goodness, faith, kindness, gentleness, and self-control. He yearns to make us more like Him so that others can see the difference that He makes and be drawn to him. God, be with people who are bitter. Help them to see you a little nearer. Amen.

Jesus said, "If you can believe, all things are possible to the one that believes" (Mark 9:23). God's Word is true. I believe Christ's Word. I can be healed through Jesus Christ, my Lord. I will always act on God's Word and rise above all doubts and fears. All things are possible to the one that believes (John 11:26). God wants us to discover that we have power over the devil and sickness.

The devil preys on the Christians. As I told you earlier about teaching the book of Revelation, the preacher told me that the devil may attack me. He doesn't like anyone that witnesses for the Lord. He doesn't like the word "Jesus." If you live according to God and His standards, be sure that your enemy is seeking to come after you. Know that God in us, and He will take care of us.

Don't blame God. When we are in despair about our frustrations, we may be tempted to blame God for our problems. "Why is God doing this to me?" God may allow Satan to tempt us, but even then, the Bible promises that God is faithful. "He will not let you be tempted beyond what you can bear" (1 Corinthians 10:13). If we fail, we have ourselves to blame. God may not necessarily be the source of the problem.

"Never blame anyone in your life. Good people give you happiness, bad people give you experience, worst people give you a lesson, and best people give you memories" (author unknown).

Know that God loves you. Never let Satan put a doubt in your mind regarding God's love for you. The devil will say, "God doesn't care," but He does because you are precious, and you are His child. Fear makes us feel weak and helpless and causes us to think we are alone in the world, but God has assured us that His spirit in us is greater than any worldly power (1 John 4:4). Whenever we become discouraged by the evil we can see, we need to think instead about the good work God is doing that we cannot see. Sickness was upon my health and symptoms of disease appeared. Satan's desire was to destroy my health.

Satan may be winning battles now but God will win the war.

> Thank You, God, for being my guide, leading me through stormy and dark paths to a place of peace that passes all understanding. Keep giving me wisdom and guidance on how to go through future storms in my life, which in turn will give me peace. Give me Your grace and strength to be committed to You even when life is full of trails. Thank You, God, for hearing me as I pray. Amen.

"God is not a man, that He should lie; Neither, the son of man, that He shall repent! As He said and shall do what He says He will do" (Numbers 23:19). Do not doubt God. If you doubt something, doubt your doubts because they are unreliable, but never doubt God or His Word. Disease takes a place among Christians today because man does not believe what God has spoken. They know God said, "I am the Lord who heals you." Believe, and He will heal you.

"I am the Lord who heals you" (Exodus 15:26). "So don't go to war without wise guidance; victory depends on having many counselors" (Proverbs 24:6). With every technological and medical discovery that occurs, God gives us new weapons to fight the physical attacks of cancer. God uses doctors and other medical professionals, trained to correctly use these weapons, as His healing agents. They are certainly a source of wise counsel in the war with cancer. Thank God for His miraculous work in our bodies through the work of the doctors and all the medical treatments you need to go through. Pray for your doctors to seek the Lord's wisdom in the treatments of your cancer. The Lord has great wisdom.

Jesus said, "If you can believe, all things are possible" (Mark 9:23). You cannot go around thinking thoughts of failure and expect God to fill you with victory. You can't go around thinking thoughts of being poor and expect God to fill you with abundance. You have to have determination; ask God for help. Talk about what God can do instead of what you can't do. God is good! He does good things for us. I really believe that God can make an example out of me. I hope people see God working in me. God created me to be in His image. God helps us, but He expects us to live in faith.

We should see ourselves as God sees us. God will help you, but you do not need to focus on negative thoughts. If you do, you are opening the door and allowing destructive attitude to dominate your life.

"Be still and know that I am God! I am exalted among the nations, I am exalted in the earth" (Psalm 46:10 NRSV). "And though you have not seen Him, you love Him, and though you do not see Him now, but believe in Him, you greatly rejoice with joy inexpressible and full of glory" (1 Peter 1:8).

Chapter 27

FAVORITE SCRIPTURES/VERSES

Ephesians 5:16. Time is more valuable than money because time is irreplaceable.

Philippians 4:13. Success comes in cans; failure comes in cant's. You can do anything through God with His help.

Proverbs 13:7. A man is rich by what he is, not by what he has. Riches are not materialistic. Rich is having God in your life. We are not rich if we have money; we are rich if we have Jesus.

Matthew 7:12. Forget yourself for others, and others will not forget you. Do unto others. Your memories will be with them forever.

Proverbs 18:9. Too many people quit looking for work when they find a job. Work hard, play hard, and rest.

Psalms 141:3. A minute of thought is worth more than an hour of talk. Listen quietly.

Ecclesiastes 9:10. What counts is not the number of hours you put in, but how much you put in the hours. Quality is more important than quantity. Work smart.

Matthew 19:26. You can accomplish more with one hour with God than one lifetime without Him. Life is so much better with God.

Luke 6:35. The best way to get even is to forget. Don't let anyone keep you in turmoil. Let them go. Don't try to get even; it will only torment you.

Philippians 4:11. Contentment is not getting what we want but being satisfied with what we have. Be happy with what you have. You are so blessed. Be happy. Happiness comes from within you. Know that it is not what we see or touch or what others do to make us happy. It is what we think, feel, and do.

"Do not be afraid, for I have ransomed you. I have called you by name; you are mine. When you go through deep waters and great trouble, I will be with you. When you go through rivers of difficulty, you will not drown" (Isaiah 43:1–2). Cancer is a major warfare. Fear attacks us and everything changes. We have new doctors and new medicine. We feel we are sinking, but know that God holds onto us and keeps us from sinking. We need to pray and ask for help and guidance.

"Show me the way in which I should walk and the things I should do" (Jeremiah 4:2–3). He will do that, and He will guide you and not let you off the path. With each step, He will reveal Himself. "Your ears shall hear a word behind you, saying, 'This is the way, walk in it'" (Isaiah 30:21). So reach up now and take God's hand. He promises He won't let you fall.

"For I can do everything with help of Christ who gives me the strength I need" (Philippians 4:13). Our battle with cancer is physically and emotionally exhausting. It pushes us to our limits and keeps us there for weeks at a time. Thankfully, we can trust God to provide whatever we need. He will give us love to reach out to a hungry friend even when we're anxious about the next lab report. He will help us be thankful even after we're finished with a difficult treatment and give us the courage to face death if we need to. Where do you need the strength of Christ to help you? Ask Him, and He will give it to you.

"God is our refuge and strength, always ready to help in times of trouble" (Psalm 46:1). God is ready to use His power to help us, but we often don't trust in His strength. Maybe it's because our natural inclination is the take care of ourselves. Maybe we're afraid that God doesn't really love us or is punishing us for some reason, but He gives us His strength simply because He loves us. One of the first steps we can take toward healing is to acknowledge our weakness and God's awesome strength. Ask Him to help you trust His love, strength, and power. Take refuge in Him when your strength is gone.

"I pray that from His glorious unlimited resources, He will give you mighty inner strength through His Holy Spirit. May your roots go down deep into the soil of God's marvelous love" (Ephesians 3:16–17). When trees go through a drought, their roots go deep into the earth in search of moisture. These deep roots provide both nourishment and stability for the tree, so the tree can flourish even in harsh circumstances. God provides His Holy Spirit for our nourishment and stability. The Holy Spirit reminds us of God's marvelous love for us and gives us the inner strength we need even during these troubled conditions. Be confident that the Holy Spirit is working on your behalf.

Prayer

> Lord, make me a path from where I am now to where I need to be. Keep me on the path You have for me and take me where You want me to go. Thank You, Lord, that You are teaching me how to walk in dependence upon You, which will be where my greatest blessing is.

The closer we walk with God, the easier it becomes. When we are faced with a difficulty and the enemy is giving us no means of escape, the Lord will open up a way out. God will fight the battle with us. Even if we lose all our strength, His strength will take over. All we have to do is pray. The battle must first be fought in the spirit before victory will be seen in the flesh by praying to God.

"You saw me before I was born. Every day of my life was recorded in your book. Every moment was laid out before a single day had passed" (Psalm 139:16).

"Yes, your healing will come quickly, your godliness will lead you forward, and the glory of the Lord will protect you from behind" (Isaiah 58:8).

"He forgives all my sins and heals all my diseases" (Psalm 103:3).

Second Peter 1:4—God's promise.

First Thessalonians 5:18. Give thanks in all circumstances, for this is the will of God in Christ Jesus for you. Have a thankful heart.

James 1:12. God will bless you if you don't give up when your faith is being tested.

Second Corinthians 4:15. We never give up. Our bodies are gradually dying, but we ourselves are being made stronger each day. You get what you give. So don't give up.

Proverbs 3:25–26. Do not be afraid of sudden panic, or of the storm that strikes the wicked; for the Lord will be your confidence.

"Brethren, I do not regard myself as having laid hold of it yet; but one thing I do: forgetting what lies behind and reaching forward to what lies ahead, I press on toward the goal for the prize of the upward call of God in Christ Jesus" (Philippians 3:13–14).

"We are pressed on every side by troubles, but we are not crushed and broken, but God never abandons us. We get knocked down, but we get up again and keep going" (2 Corinthians 4:8–9). At times, it seems like the treatments for cancer is worse than the cancer itself.

Proverbs 3:5–6. Joy is the deep seated confidence that God is in control of very area of your life. When I was facing the tough times, I tried to not lose my joy because I knew that God is in control, and I believed strongly that He can take my problem and turn it around and use it to my advantage.

Psalm 41:22, Jeremiah 31:13. God knows how to turn things around. He can turn your sorrow into joy. Just let Him in.

Hebrews 13:8, Malachi 3:6. Jesus Christ, the same yesterday and today and forever. When you appreciate God's blessing, you will be able in difficult times. If He blessed me before, He'll do it again.

Romans 8:28. If you're struggling to see God's purpose in your suffering today, rest assured He has one. When you trust Him, He makes all things work together for good. Difficult roads lead to beautiful destinations.

Isaiah 65:24. You can start thanking God today for what He will do for you tomorrow because He will—absolutely will—come through for you. Never be a prisoner of your past. It was just a lesson, not a life sentence.

"Blessed is the man who trust in the Lord, whose confidence is in Him. He will be like a tree planted by the water that send out its roots by the stream. It does not fear. When heat comes, it's leaves are always green. It has no worries in a year of drought and never fails to bear fruit" (Jeremiah 17:7–8).

Psalm 119:105, Matthew 19:17. Contentment and fulfillment are achieved when we walk straight along the path the Lord has set before us.

Job 11:18. Regardless of your circumstances, keep your joy alive today by staying focused on God!

"The Lord is my strength and my shield, my heart trusted in Him, and I am helped. Therefore, my heart greatly rejoices and with my glory, I will praise Him" (Psalm 28:7).

"So do not fear for I am with you; do not be dismayed, for I am your God. I will strengthen you and help you; I will uphold you with my righteous right hand" (Isaiah 41:10 NIV).

"Have not I commanded thee? Be strong and of a good courage; be not afraid, neither be thou dismayed: for the Lord thy God is with thee whithersoever thou goest" (Joshua 1:9).

"The Lord is my light and my salvation; whom shall I fear? The Lord is the strength of my life; of whom shall I be afraid?" (Psalm 27:1).

"For God hath not given us the spirit of fear; but of power, and of love, and of a sound mind" (2 Timothy 1:7).

These are things that I have learned:

- I have learned your wrong thinking can keep you from God's best. Try to have a positive attitude.
- I have learned you must conceive it in your heart and mind before you can receive it. Have a relationship with the Lord.
- I have learned that God meets us at our level of expectancy. He takes care of us.
- I have learned that this could be the day I see a miracle from my good Lord. He heals us.
- I have learned that what I will receive is directly connected to how I believe. Have faith.
- I have learned if you change your thinking, God can change your life. Pray and seek Him.
- I have learned if you do your part then God will do His part. He will open doors for you. If you transform your mind, God will transform your life. Believe in Him.
- I have learned to not focus on my weakness. I must focus on God. Trust Him.
- I have learned to see myself as a winner and an overcomer. Be confident in yourself.
- I have learned to be happy with who God made me to be. Love yourself.
- I have learned that what I believe has a much greater impact on my life than what anybody else believes. Have faith in God.
- I have learned that when I think positive, I will go toward greatness.
- I have learned to bless and witness to anyone I can. I want to witness for my Lord always.
- I have learned a bitter root will produce bitter fruit. Don't be negative.
- I have learned you cannot put a question mark where God has put a period. Quit questioning God and trust Him.
- I have learned God works the most when we see it and feel it the least. Have faith.

- I have learned that you would not be so concerned about what people thought of you if you knew how seldom they did.
- I have learned to not worry about things I can't change. Read the Serenity Prayer.
- I have learned that God's people are the happiness people on earth. Christians are happy.
- I have learned that I'm too blessed to be stressed. You are blessed.
- I have learned that the battle is His; the victory is mine; He will help me win the race. He works miracles.
- I have learned to fear not, for He is with me (Isaiah 41:10). Do not worry or be afraid. He is with you.
- I have learned to trust in God's healing, timing, and plan. He healed me in His timing and His plan.
- I have learned all things work together for good to them that love the Lord. Love the Lord, and you will always have support from Him.
- I have learned that God guides me, protects me, and keeps me in His perfect will.
- I have learned this the tough times of my life that I find out what I'm really made of. We are just as indispensable as anyone else, but we can get through it with the Lord's help

Thank You, Lord, for surrounding us with Your peace. Keep us aware of Your constant presence regardless of the circumstances. Thank You for those that have touched our life and helped us grow in Your grace. Lord, help us to stand strong in our faith to You. Thank You for fighting our battles and protecting us from the evil one. Strengthen us as we study Your Word and apply it to our life daily. Thank you for all your blessings and miracles you have given us. In your name we pray. Amen.

I pray this book has been a blessing for you as much as it has been for me writing it. Always know you can Fear Not, because He is with you and always will be.

About the Author

Brenda has been blessed, and she says she owes it all to the good Lord for His blessings and miracles. She has been through a variety of obstacles in her life, but through it all, she let go and let God. She went through cancer in 2009, which was very hard. While going through the difficulties, she kept her faith through it all when the doctors did not give hope. She was an inspiration to everyone that came around her at that time. The Lord gave her hope and healing through His perfect timing and plan. As of today, she is healthy and happy, enjoying her life with her family, whom she is so proud of.

Brenda has always put others before herself. She is a caregiver and mentor. She always loves to inspire and give hope to her family and friends at a time of crises. She wanted her children to know the Lord as she does.

While her children were in high school, she sent them to a Christian School so they could keep growing with the Lord's Word. At that time, she did not know how she was going to be able to afford it. She put it in the Lord's hand and prayed about it. The Lord was good. Soon after she enrolled them, her daughter came home and said there was an opening in the business office, and they wanted her to go apply for it. She got the job working at the Christian School. That was the Lord's giving a pathway for her to be able to send them. By working there, the tuition was paid for. She worked there ten years and enjoyed working with the staff and children.

While she was going through her cancer, she promised she would always witness and tell everyone what miracles God has blessed her and her family with. There are three things she wants to do, and those are…

1. To praise Him and give Him glory.
2. To witness to others His blessings and healing power.
3. To put Him in the lives of her family, children, and grandchildren.

As part of her witnessing, she has written this book and has spoken at several churches giving her testimonies. She loved writing this book so everyone can get a blessing out of it. It will give you hope when needed, encouragement when needed, and peace when needed. Trust in the Lord and have faith in His Word.

Below are pictures of my four grandchildren whom, I love with all my heart.

Top, left to right: Dalton and Tucker. Bottom,
left to right: Alexis and George Michael